MW01032539

Backyard
Wildlife

Written and Illustrated
by Todd Telander

FALCONGUIDES

GUILFORD, CONNECTICUT
HELENA, MONTANA

AN IMPRINT OF ROWMAN & LITTLEFIELD

To my wife Kirsten, my children Miles and Oliver, and my parents—
all of whom have supported and encouraged me through the years

FALCONGUIDES®

An imprint of Rowman & Littlefield

Distributed by NATIONAL BOOK NETWORK

Copyright © 2015 Rowman & Littlefield
Illustrations © 2015 Todd Telander

Falcon, FalconGuides, and Outfit Your Mind are registered trademarks of Rowman & Littlefield.

British Library Cataloguing-in-Publication Information available
Library of Congress Cataloging-in-Publication Data available

ISBN 978-1-4930-0630-4 (paperback)

♾™ The paper used in this publication meets the minimum requirements of
American National Standard for Information Sciences—Permanence of Paper
for Printed Library Materials, ANSI/NISO Z39.48-1992.

Contents

Introduction

Our homes and yards are habitat not only for humans, but also for a wide array of wild creatures. Taking the time to learn about some of these inhabitants can be a rewarding experience, as much so as taking a trip to a national park or wildlife refuge. Surrounding us, even in urban settings, are animals that accept, or even benefit, from the presence of human existence and the changes we have made to the environment. Mammals, birds, reptiles, amphibians, and a host of insects and other invertebrates are part of our daily lives but often go unnoticed. This guide is intended to encourage you to identify and learn about our wild cohabitants, wherever you may live. Let your exploration begin, whether you want to know about the birds that visit your feeder, the spiders that spin beautiful webs in your garden, the raccoons that knock over your trash cans, the squirrels that dance through the trees, or the frogs that chirp in spring.

Notes about the Species Accounts

Names

Both the common and scientific names are included for each entry. Since common names tend to vary regionally, and there may be more than one common name for each species, the universally accepted scientific name of genus and species (such as *Passer domesticus* for the House Sparrow) is a reliable way to be certain of identification. Also, you can learn interesting facts about an animal by understanding the English translation of its Latin name. For instance, the generic name *passer* means "a type of sparrow," and *domesticus* means "of the home."

Size

Most measurements of size refer to overall length, from nose to tail tip. For animals with very long tails, antennae, or other appendages, measurements for those parts may be given separately from those of the body. Butterfly and moth measurements refer to wingspan. Size may vary considerably within a species (due to age, sex, or environmental conditions), so use this measurement as a general guide, not a rule.

Range

Range refers to the geographical area where a species is likely to be found, such as Pacific Northwest, Southwest, eastern United States, throughout North America, etc. Some species may be found throughout their range, whereas others prefer very specific habitats within the range. Animals may also have different ranges depending on the time of year, such as birds and butterflies that migrate.

Habitat

An animal's habitat is one of the first clues to its identification. Note the environment (including vegetation, climate, elevation, substrate, presence or absence of water) and compare it with the description listed for the animal. Some common habitats include prairies, pine forests, alpine meadows, tundra, foothills, sage lands, chaparral, rivers and streams, urban areas, and grasslands. The proximity of your home and yard to these habitats will influence what wildlife you can expect to find.

Illustrations

The illustrations show adult animals in their most common coloration and form. Many species show variation in different geographical areas, in different seasons, or between the sexes. Birds, many insects, and some spiders show this variety most often, and I have generally mentioned the specifics in the text.

Useful Scientific Terms

I have, for the most part, used familiar language to describe the animals in this book, but there are occasions when it makes more sense to use terms developed by the scientific community, especially when referring to body parts. In particular, terms and characteristics associated with birds, reptiles, amphibians, general insects, and butterflies are described below:

Birds

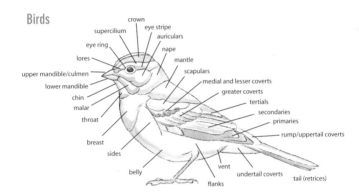

crown
supercilium
eye stripe
auriculars
eye ring
nape
lores
mantle
upper mandible/culmen
scapulars
lower mandible
medial and lesser coverts
chin
greater coverts
malar
tertials
throat
secondaries
primaries
breast
rump/uppertail coverts
sides
belly
vent
undertail coverts
flanks
tail (retrices)

Lizards

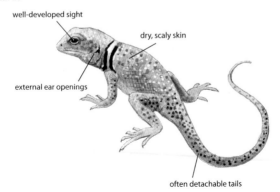

well-developed sight
dry, scaly skin
external ear openings
often detachable tails

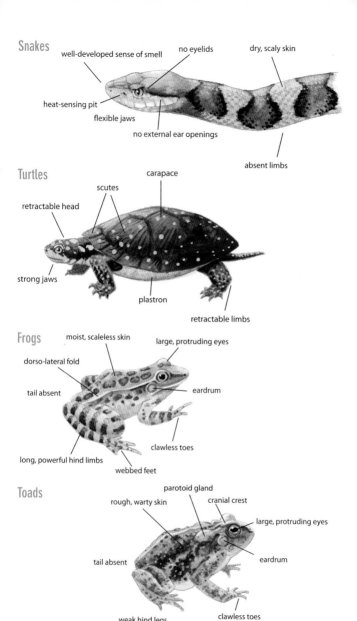

Snakes

- well-developed sense of smell
- no eyelids
- dry, scaly skin
- heat-sensing pit
- flexible jaws
- no external ear openings
- absent limbs

Turtles

- carapace
- scutes
- retractable head
- strong jaws
- plastron
- retractable limbs

Frogs

- moist, scaleless skin
- large, protruding eyes
- dorso-lateral fold
- tail absent
- eardrum
- clawless toes
- long, powerful hind limbs
- webbed feet

Toads

- parotoid gland
- rough, warty skin
- cranial crest
- large, protruding eyes
- tail absent
- eardrum
- weak hind legs
- clawless toes

Salamanders

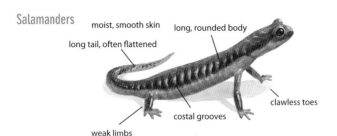

moist, smooth skin
long, rounded body
long tail, often flattened
clawless toes
costal grooves
weak limbs

Butterflies

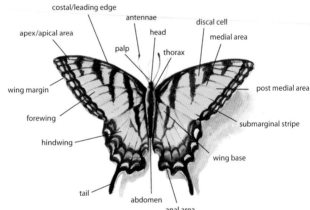

costal/leading edge
antennae
discal cell
apex/apical area
head
medial area
palp
thorax
wing margin
post medial area
forewing
submarginal stripe
hindwing
wing base
tail
abdomen
anal area

Beetles

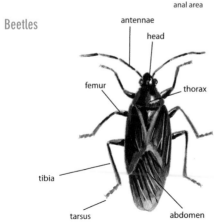

antennae
head
femur
thorax
tibia
tarsus
abdomen

MAMMALS

Virginia Opossum, *Didelphis virginiana*
Family Didelphidae (Opossums)
Size: 30" with tail
Range: Central and eastern United States; portions of Pacific states
Habitat: Woodlands, riparian zones, urban areas with trees, farms
The Virginia Opossum is a marsupial, meaning it bears premature young that develop in an external pouch, and is the only member of this group in North America. It is stocky, with relatively small limbs, a pointed snout, and a long, round, hairless tail. Its color is mottled grayish, with a white face and dark ears. It is nocturnal, mostly solitary, and reasonably adept at swimming and climbing. It has a highly varied diet that includes nuts, fruit, insects, small animals, and carrion. Opossums have a curious habit of feigning death when under attack, then resuming as normal once safe.

Southern Short-tailed Shrew, *Blarina carolinensis*
Family Soricidae (Shrews)
Size: 3-5" long with tail
Range: Southeastern United States
Habitat: Moist woodlands, brushy areas

Shrews are the smallest mammals in North America and are unrelated to the rodents. The Southern Short-tailed Shrew is very active. It is shaped like a long mouse, with a sharply pointed head, tiny eyes, no external ears, and a short, lightly furred tail. Its fur is dense, dark gray above and slightly paler below. This shrew is active day and night, mostly solitary, and utilizes an extensive network of tunnels, which it digs itself. Voracious feeders, shrews forage within their tunnels and nearby leaf litter for insects, earthworms, spiders, small invertebrates, and sometimes nuts and seeds. Shrews can also secrete poisonous saliva that paralyzes prey.

Eastern Mole, *Scalopus aquaticus*
Family Talpidae (True Moles)
Size: 6" long with tail
Range: Central and eastern United States
Habitat: A variety, including fields, woodlands, lawns, and areas with dry, loose soils

Also known as the Common Mole, the Eastern Mole is a small, stocky, sturdy mammal with a body well designed for life underground. It is elongate and tube-shaped, with narrow hips, a pointed, fleshy snout, and a short tail. Its fur is short, velvety, deep gray brown above and slightly paler below. Its eyes are tiny and covered by skin, and its ears are invisible beneath its fur. Eastern Moles build tunnels, which they dig with their broad, spade-like forelimbs and long, thick claws. They forage within the tunnels for earthworms, insects, and some plants. Eastern moles are responsible for creating conspicuous dirt mounds at the entrances to their tunnels.

Big Brown Bat, *Eptesicus fuscus*
Family Vespertilionidae (Vespertilionid Bats)
Size: 5" with tail
Range: Throughout the contiguous United States
Habitat: A wide variety, including woodlands, buildings, and caves

As a group, bats are the only mammals that truly fly, using wings made of a thin membrane stretched across elongate forearms and fingers. The Big Brown Bat is widely distributed. It is fairly large, with fur that is brown above and lighter below, with blackish wing membranes. There is a fleshy projection at the base of the ear (the tragus), which is short and rounded. Big Brown Bats are nocturnal, roosting by day in dark, secluded areas such as caves or old buildings. They emerge at night to forage for beetles and other insects, locating them primarily by echolocation, emitting high-pitched chirps and receiving reflected sound with their complex, large ears.

Brazilian Free-tailed Bat, *Tadarida brasiliensis*
Family Molossidae (Free-Tailed Bats)
Size: ~4" with tail
Range: Throughout the contiguous United States
Habitat: Caves, buildings, and surrounding environs
Also known as the Mexican Free-tailed Bat or Guano Bat, the Brazilian Free-tailed Bat is small, with narrow wings and a tail that projects freely about halfway past the interfemoral membrane, a patch of skin that stretches between the legs. Its fur is rich brown, slightly darker above than below, and its wings are blackish. The ears are broad, reaching forward on the face, and the upper snout is wrinkled. Brazilian free-tailed bats emerge from roosting sites at night in large groups and forage in the air for a variety of insects, using echolocation to zero in on prey. These bats are among the most numerous mammals in the United States, famous for gathering in enormous concentrations in caves in New Mexico and for depositing deep accumulations of guano in those caves.

Black-tailed Jackrabbit, *Lepus californicus*
Family Leporidae (Rabbits and Hares)
Size: ~23" long
Range: Western United States
Habitat: Prairies, open sage land, meadows

The black-tailed jackrabbit is a large, lanky hare with relatively long legs and huge, black-tipped ears. The color is gray brown, paler underneath, with a white tail that has a black stripe on top that extends onto the rump. The similar white-tailed jackrabbit has no dark upper surface on the tail and inhabits the mountains of eastern California. Jackrabbits are mostly nocturnal and solitary, highly alert, and able to elude predators with exceptionally fast runs and high jumps. They forage on grass and other vegetation, but may be limited to bark and buds in winter.

Eastern Cottontail, *Sylvilagus floridanus*
Family Leporidae (Rabbits and Hares)
Size: 15" long
Range: East of the Continental Divide
Habitat: Open woodlands, areas near water, dense brush

The Eastern Cottontail is colored gray brown to reddish brown, with a short, rounded, white tail (hence the common name). Its eyes are quite large, and its rear feet are long and powerful. Like other rabbits, they are an important food source for most carnivorous wildlife. Eastern Cottontails are mostly nocturnal, but can be seen feeding at almost any time for grasses, herbs, branches, and bark. They never stay too far from brushy cover or their burrows. They are almost identical to the Desert Cottontail of western states, but are a bit larger with proportionately smaller ears.

Brush Rabbit, *Sylvilagus bachmani*
Family Leporidae (Rabbits and Hares)
Size: 13"
Range: Pacific United States
Habitat: Dense, brushy areas
The Brush Rabbit is a smaller version of the desert cottontail, with a preference for thick brush in which to hide. Its fur is coarse; the color is brownish gray overall. Its ears are relatively small, and the tail is grayish brown and inconspicuous, unlike the white of the cottontail. Brush Rabbits are secretive, foraging mostly during the night on all matter of vegetation, including twigs, grasses, bulbs, tubers, and leaves. As a defense they remain motionless, or run for the cover of brush, tunnels, or trees, and may be heard thumping their hind legs on the ground.

Western Gray Squirrel, *Sciurus griseus*
Family Sciuridae (Squirrels)
Size: 18" with tail
Range: Pacific United States
Habitat: Mixed hardwood forests, parks, suburbs

The widespread and common Western Gray Squirrel, also known as the California Gray Squirrel, is social, arboreal, and relatively large. It has a long, very bushy tail and large eyes. Its color is gray, sometimes with a brownish cast, and whitish below, with pale eye rings. Its tail is edged with white-tipped hairs. Active most times of the day, these squirrels forage for nuts, fruits, seeds, insects, eggs, and fungi, and may store nuts in ground caches. Ubiquitous in rural yards and parks, they use tree cavities to nest in or may build large nests of twigs and leaves high in a tree.

Northern Flying Squirrel, *Glaucomys sabrinus*
Family Sciuridae (Squirrels)
Size: 16" with tail
Range: Northern United States
Habitat: Coniferous or deciduous woodlands, oak stands

The Northern Flying Squirrel is small and unusual, designed to glide (not fly) from tree to tree or from tree to ground. Flaps of skin connect the front and rear feet; when outstretched, these flaps allow the squirrel to glide more than 100 feet and make a delicate landing. The color is grayish brown, darker along the flanks, and whitish below. These squirrels are active at night and are highly social, with several individuals sometimes sharing a nest site in a tree cavity or external structure. They forage for nuts, fruit, insects, fungus, and eggs and store food in tree cavities for winter use.

Eastern Fox Squirrel, *Sciurus niger*
Family Sciuridae (Squirrels)
Size: 24–30" long with tail
Range: Central and eastern United States
Habitat: Open, mature woodlands

The Eastern Fox Squirrel is a large tree squirrel with a long, bushy tail. It occurs in variable color morphs: The body can be rusty brown to grayish to all black above, with the underside whitish or tawny. In Colorado the fox squirrel is usually reddish brown on the back and sides and pale orange on the belly, face, and legs. Eastern Fox Squirrels are generally solitary, searching in trees or on the ground for nuts, buds, and berries. In the fall, they cache nuts in tree cavities or in large nests in the crotches of trees, which the squirrels construct from leaves.

California Ground Squirrel, *Otospermophilus beecheyi*
Family Sciuridae (Squirrels)
Size: About 18" with tail
Range: Western United States
Habitat: Fields, open woodlands, rocky area

The California Ground Squirrel is fairly common in open spaces throughout the far western states. These squirrels are of medium length with bushy tails. The fur is speckled in shades of brown, gray, and white, with a darker, forward-pointing V-shaped patch along the back and whitish patches along the sides to the base of the neck. The underside is paler, there are prominent white eye rings, and the tail is mottled or striped in the body colors. These squirrels are active during the day, sunning themselves or foraging for a wide variety of food, including nuts, seeds, berries, roots, and insects. They form loose colonies with extensive bur-row systems, which they excavate, and each individual has its own entrance, to which it will retreat to when in danger.

Least Chipmunk, *Tamias minimus*
Family Sciuridae (Squirrels)
Size: ~8" with tail
Range: Western United States
Habitat: Arid, high-elevation open forests to lowland sagebrush and rocky areas

The smallest chipmunk in North America, but similar in body shape to other chipmunks, the Least Chipmunk has a small body, large head and eyes, and a long, bushy tail. The most obvious field marks are the white-and-dark brown stripes across the head and along the back. Much geographical variation exists, but typically the Least Chipmunk's sides are orange-brown, the underparts are pale gray, and the tail is mottled in the body colors, often striped with black near the base. The chipmunk usually holds its tail in a vertical position when running. Least Chipmunks are active during the day from spring to fall, busily collecting nuts, berries, grasses, and insects, using an extendable cheek pouch to carry extra food for storage. They nest in burrows, under logs, or in trees and spend the winter in partial hibernation underground, where they periodically awaken to nibble on bits of cached food. These chipmunks often visit campsites for food and can be quite vocal, emitting a high-pitched *chip*. The similar Colorado Chipmunk is larger, with longer stripes on the back.

Red Squirrel, *Tamiasciurus hudsonicus*
Family Sciuridae (Squirrels)
Size: ~12" long with tail
Range: Northeastern United States, intermountain west
Habitat: Coniferous or mixed woodlands

The Red Squirrel, also known as the Pine Squirrel and the Chickaree, is feisty, highly territorial, and most at home in trees. It is relatively small, with a bushy tail and large eyes encircled with white. The color is reddish brown above and white below, with a dark band in between. These squirrels may be somewhat paler in winter months. They are primarily active during the day and at all times of the year. They eat the nuts of pine and spruce cones, but they will also eat berries, insects, and mushrooms.

American Beaver, *Castor canadensis*
Family Castoridae (Beavers)
Size: 28" body; 10" tail
Range: Throughout the United States
Habitat: Ponds, lakes, streams with adjacent woodlands
Once nearly extirpated because of hunting and trapping for pelts, this largest of North American rodents now covers most of its original range. The beaver is heavy and compact, with webbed rear feet, large front incisors, and a long, dexterous, scaled, flattened tail. The color is dark brown. Beavers are known for cooperative construction of impressive dams and lodges made from trees they have felled. Their presence is often announced by loud tail slaps on the water. Mostly nocturnal, beavers eat the tender, inner bark of trees, as well as small branches and buds.

Ord's Kangaroo Rat, *Dipodomys ordii*
Family Heteromyidae (Pocket Mice, Kangaroo Mice, and Kangaroo Rats)
Size: ~ 4" body; 5½" tail
Range: Inland western United States
Habitat: Lowland prairies and scrublands with sandy soils

One of several species of kangaroo rats across the arid west, the Ord's Kangaroo Rat occupies the largest range and is one of the smaller varieties. It is a compact rodent with a relatively large head, a long tail with a bushy distal portion, and oversize rear feet, akin to a kangaroo. Its color is buff to rusty brown, with white lateral stripes across the lower body and the middle of the tail. Mostly nocturnal and somewhat solitary, kangaroo rats spend the day in their burrows. They hop about, kangaroo-style, foraging for plants, seeds, and insects. They are well adapted to dry conditions and receive most of the water they need through their food.

Eastern Wood Rat, *Neotoma floridana*
Family Cricetidae (New World Mice and Rats)
Size: 21" long with tail
Range: Eastern and central United States
Habitat: Grasslands, woodlands, rural buildings

The Eastern Wood Rat is a chunky, large rodent with a squarish head, large ears, and hairy tail that is usually slightly shorter than its body. The fur is grayish brown above, with white below and on the feet. Eastern Wood Rats are nocturnal, breed year-round, and feed on plant matter and seeds, as well as fungi. They build house-like nests of sticks and debris in crevices, burrows, or caves, which offer protection and a place to cache food. They are members of the "pack rat" group, known to collect bits of small metallic refuse.

Deer Mouse, *Peromyscus maniculatus*
Family Cricetidae (New World Mice and Rats)
Size: 4" body; 3" tail
Range: Throughout the United States except for the far south
Habitat: Highly variable: grasslands, woodlands, mountains, brushlands
The Deer Mouse is common and widespread. It occurs in a wide range of habitats, and can vary in size and color depending on region. The appearance is typical of the mice, with a small body, pointed snout, large, black eyes, and large ears. The tail is thin and varies in length, but is typically slightly shorter than the body. Color ranges from grayish to brown or orange-brown above, with a white underside and lower part of the face. The tail is dark above, sharply contrasting with white below. Deer Mice are most commonly active during the night, emerging from daytime refuges of burrows or under rocks and stumps. They scamper along the ground, in brush, or in trees gathering nuts, fruits, grasses, and insects. They store extra food to eat during lean winter months in a hidden cache, since they do not hibernate.

Porcupine, *Erethizon dorsatum*
Family Erethizontidae (Porcupines)
Size: ~28" with tail
Range: Western and far northeastern United States
Habitat: Forests, thickets
The Porcupine is a primarily arboreal, chunky, lackadaisical rodent with small limbs, a bushy tail, and thousands of pointed barbed quills, which serve as its only defense. Its color is dark brown to blackish. Found alone or in groups, the Porcupine is mostly nocturnal but can be seen at all times of the day, often perched in trees. Porcupines feed on all types of plant matter, including buds, branches, bark, roots, and leaves.

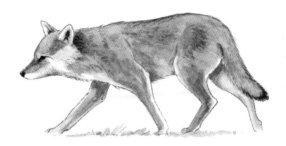

Coyote, *Canis latrans*
Family Canidae (Coyotes, Wolves, and Foxes)
Size: 4' with tail
Range: Throughout most of the United States except the southeastern region
Habitat: Open country, scrub, grasslands

The Coyote is an intelligent and adaptable canid that has been able to survive in a wide variety of habitats and in spite of persecution by humans. It looks like an average-size dog, with a long, thin muzzle and pointed ears. The color can range from gray to light brown or reddish. It has a bushy tail that is held low or between the legs. Coyotes hunt alone or in small packs, primarily during the night. Their diet is varied, and they scavenge for anything edible, including rodents, rabbits, snakes, berries, insects, and carrion.

Gray Fox, *Urocyon cinereoargenteus*
Family Canidae (Coyotes, Wolves, and Foxes)
Size: 3' with tail
Range: Throughout most of the contiguous United States except parts of northwestern and north-central states
Habitat: Open woodlands, brush, suburban areas
The Gray Fox is a small, stealthy, nimble canid with a bushy tail and the ability to climb trees using its short, curved, retractable claws. Its fur is gray and white speckled above and reddish along the sides and legs, and there is a black streak down the back and tail, ending in a black tail tip. Its muzzle is thin and small, while its ears are comparatively large. Gray Foxes are mostly solitary and nocturnal and feed on a varied diet that includes rabbits, rodents, insects, nuts, and fruit.

Red Fox, *Vulpes vulpes*
Family Canidae (Coyotes, Wolves, and Foxes)
Size: 38" with tail
Range: Throughout most of the contiguous United States; Alaska
Habitat: Open woodlands, fields, brushy areas; may approach urban centers
Like other foxes, the Red Fox is wily, secretive, adaptable, and dog-like. It has a small muzzle, large ears, and a bushy tail. It is rusty red above, white or gray below, with black "stockings" on its legs and a white-tipped tail. Color variations may include black or slate gray, and the fox may have a dark cross along the shoulders. Red Foxes are solitary hunters and are most active at night or in the twilight hours, seeking the shelter of a den during the day. They feed on small mammals, insects, carrion, plants, and berries, sometimes performing a dramatic leaping pounce to catch rodents.

Raccoon, *Procyon lotor*
Family Procyonidae (Ringtails and Raccoons)
Size: 34" with tail
Range: Throughout most of the contiguous United States
Habitat: Woodlands, streams or lakesides, urban areas

The Raccoon is a highly adaptable mammal, equally at home in remote forests or urban centers. It is stocky and heavy, with a short, masked face and a bushy coat. Its color is pale gray mixed with black, with a tail ringed in black and gray. Incredibly dexterous fingers allow it to undo knots and even work doorknobs. Raccoon are primarily nocturnal and may be seen alone or in small groups. They prefer to feed near a water source, often dipping their food in water first, and will eat just about anything, including fruit, nuts, insects, fish, crayfish, and worms.

Long-tailed Weasel, *Mustela frenata*
Family Mustelidae (Weasels and Otters)
Size: 14" with tail
Range: Throughout the contiguous United States
Habitat: Woodlands, fields with brushy cover, often found near water

The Long-tailed Weasel is a wily, small, elongate, long-necked predator and one of North America's smallest meat eaters. It is reddish brown, with buff-colored underparts and throat, and has a black tip on its long tail. The weasel is nocturnal and solitary, is an excellent climber, and, due to its thin, sinuous shape and short legs, can slip into burrows to attack rodents living within. Long-tailed Weasels also hunt rabbits, birds, eggs, and fish. To den, they use the existing burrows of similar-size rodents.

Striped Skunk, *Mephitis mephitis*
Family Mephitidae (Skunks)
Size: 22" with tail
Range: Throughout the contiguous United States
Habitat: Woodlands, brush, suburban parks; usually near a water source
The Striped Skunk is known primarily for its ability to elude danger by spraying a noxious fluid from an anal duct. It is a stocky, weasel-like mammal with a long, bushy tail and long front claws for digging. Its color is black, with broad white stripes running down its sides that merge into a white stripe on the upper part of the tail. Usually solitary, Striped Skunks stay in dens during the day and forage at night. Being omnivorous, they eat a wide variety of foods including fruit, nuts, insects, small mammals, and eggs.

Western Spotted Skunk, *Spilogale gracilis*
Family Mephitidae (Skunks)
Size: 18" with tail
Range: Western United States
Habitat: Brushy open woodlands, coastal scrub, grasslands; usually near a water source

The Western Spotted Skunk is smaller than the Striped Skunk but shares its defensive ability to spray a noxious liquid from ducts near its anus. It is weasel-like, with fine soft fur, a thick bushy tail, and long claws. Its color is black, with variable and irregular white spotting and striping on its head and back, and it has a white-tipped tail. Solitary and nocturnal, these skunks stay in dens during the day. They can climb trees but mostly forage on the ground, eating a variety of foods, including fruit, insects, small mammals, birds, and eggs. The very similar Eastern Spotted Skunk lives east of the Rocky Mountains.

Mountain Lion, *Puma concolor*
Family Felidae (Cats)
Size: 7' body; 2½' tail (males larger than females)
Range: Western United States; western Gulf states; Florida
Habitat: Open to dense woodlands, brush

The Mountain Lion (also known as the Cougar or Puma) is a huge (about 125 pounds), reclusive, powerful cat. It has a long tail, and its fur is a blend of tawny browns, tans, and grays, paler on the underside and white on the chest and throat. The tail tip is dark brown, as are the backs of the ears and marks on the muzzle. Mountain Lions are mostly solitary, except during breeding season or when mothers are with kittens. They hunt by stealth, waiting on rocky ledges or in trees for prey to pass or slinking through grass to ambush prey, which includes deer, elk, and smaller mammals.

Bobcat, *Lynx rufus*
Family Felidae (Cats)
Size: 28" body; 5" tail
Range: Throughout most of the contiguous United States except for parts of the east-central region
Habitat: A wide variety of habitats, including forests, riparian areas, scrub

The Bobcat is about double the size of a housecat, is well camouflaged, and has a very short "bobbed" tail. Its face appears wide due to long fur tufts below its ears, and the ears are tipped with short black hairs. The color is light brown to reddish above, pale or whitish below, and spotted with dark brown or black that sometimes is streaked on the animal's legs. The tail is striped and black along the top edge. Bobcats are typically active during the early morning and after dusk; in winter they are active during the day. They hunt by stealth, ambushing their favored prey of rabbits, other small mammals, and birds. The similar lynx is a bit larger and has an all-black tail.

Mule Deer, *Odocoileus hemionus*
Family Cervidae (Deer, Elk, and Moose)
Size: 6' long with tail (males larger than females)
Range: Central and western United States
Habitat: Quite variable; forests, chaparral, bushy grasslands
The Mule Deer is quite common throughout its range and so-called because of its very large mule-like ears. Its color is gray brown in winter, rusty brown in summer, with a white throat, muzzle, and belly. Depending on the region, its tail may have a black tip or may have black on the top surface. Males have antlers that are evenly forked (not with tines from a central beam, as in the white-tailed deer). In summer the antlers are covered in velvet. Mule deer are active at twilight, moving in small groups or singly and browsing for tree branches, grasses, and herbs.

White-tailed Deer, *Odocoileus virginianus*
Family Cervidae (Deer, Elk, and Moose)
Size: 6' body; 10" tail
Range: Most of the contiguous United States except for much of California, Nevada, and Utah
Habitat: Dense forest, forest edges

North America's smallest deer, the White-tailed Deer is a secretive mammal of thick forests. It is very agile, fast, and able to outmaneuver most predators. The male has antlers with a main beam that supports smaller prongs. The color of its fur is reddish brown, with a white belly and throat. When alarmed, the White-tailed Deer raises its tail, revealing the brilliant white underside, hence its colloquial name of "flagtail." White-tailed Deer travel in small groups in summer, but in winter they may congregate in larger herds. Being herbivores, they forage for grasses, herbs, and nuts.

BIRDS

Canada Goose, *Branta canadensis*
Family Anatidae (Geese, Ducks, and Mergansers)
Size: 27–35" depending on race
Range: Throughout the United States
Habitat: Marshes, grasslands, public parks, golf courses

The Canada Goose is the most common goose in the United States and is found in suburban settings. It is vegetarian, foraging on land for grass, seeds, and grain or in the water by upending like the dabbling ducks. It has a heavy body with short, thick legs and a long neck. Overall its coloring is barred gray brown, with a white rear, a short black tail, a black neck, and a white patch running from under the neck to behind the eye. During its powerful flight, the goose's white rump makes a semicircular patch between the tail and back. Its voice is a loud honk. In flight Canada Geese form the classic V formation. The adult is illustrated.

Mute Swan, *Cygnus olor*
Family Anatidae (Geese, Ducks, Mergansers)
Size: 60"
Range: Northeastern United States
Habitat: Ponds, lakes, coastal bays; usually in or near developed areas

Native to northern Europe and central Asia, the Mute Swan was introduced in the early 1900s to parks and gardens of the eastern United States. It is a large, graceful swan that holds its neck in a smooth curve and has a relatively long pointed tail and uniformly white plumage. The face is black in front of the eyes, meeting with a reddish orange bill and a black, bulbous knob at the forehead. Although mostly quiet, it is capable of a range of hisses, snorts, and loud nasal calls. Mute Swans forage for aquatic plants and can be quite aggressive, often displaying a posture with the head tilted down and the wings raised over the back. It is a species of concern, because as its range expands it displaces many native birds. The adult is illustrated.

Wood Duck, *Aix sponsa*
Family Anatidae (Geese, Ducks, Mergansers)
Size: 18"
Range: Most of the contiguous United States except for the southwestern region
Habitat: Wooded ponds and swamps

The regal Wood Duck is among the dabbling ducks, or those that tip headfirst into shallow water to pluck aquatic plants and animals from the bottom. The male is long tailed and small billed and shows a dark back, light buff flanks, and sharp black-and-white head patterning. It also sports a bushy head crest that droops behind the nape. The female is gray brown with spotting along the underside and a conspicuous white teardrop-shaped eye patch. Both sexes swim with their heads angled downward as if in a nod and have sharp claws, which they use to cling to branches and snags. The breeding female (top) and breeding male are illustrated.

Mallard, *Anas platyrhynchos*
Family Anatidae (Geese, Ducks, and Mergansers)
Size: 23"
Range: Throughout the United States
Habitat: Parks and urban areas; virtually any environment with water

The ubiquitous Mallard is the most abundant duck in the Northern Hemisphere. It is a classic dabbling duck, plunging its head into the water with its tail up, searching for aquatic plants, animals, and snails. It will also eat worms, seeds, insects, and even mice. Noisy and quacking, it is heavy but a strong flier. The male has a dark head with green or blue iridescence, a white neck ring, and a large yellow bill. His underparts are pale, with a chestnut-brown breast. The female is plain brownish, with buff-colored, scalloped markings. She also has a dark eye line and an orangey bill with a dark center. The speculum is blue on both sexes, and the tail coverts often curl upward. Mallards form huge floating flocks called "rafts." To achieve flight, the mallard lifts straight into the air without running. The breeding male, below, and a female, above, are illustrated.

Ruddy Duck, *Oxyura jamaicensis*

Family Anatidae (Geese, Ducks, and Mergansers)
Size: 15"
Range: Throughout the United States
Habitat: Open water, wetlands

The Ruddy Duck is a "stiff-tailed duck," part of a group known for rigid tail feathers that are often cocked up in display. It dives deep for its food, which consists of aquatic vegetation, and flies low over the water with quick wing beats. A relatively small duck, with a big head and a flat, broad body, the breeding male is a rich sienna brown overall, with white cheeks, a black cap and nape, and a bright blue bill. The female is drab, with a conspicuous dark stripe across her cheek. Nonbreeding males become gray. The Ruddy Duck can sink low into the water, grebe-like, and will often dive to escape danger. The breeding male, below, and a female, above, are illustrated.

Ring-necked Pheasant, *Phasianus colchicus*

Family Phasianidae (Pheasants, Grouse, and Turkeys)
Size: 21" (male), 34" (female)
Range: Mostly higher latitudes across the United States, south to Texas
Habitat: Grasslands, woodland edges, agricultural land with brushy cover

The Ring-necked Pheasant is a large chicken-shaped bird with a long pointed tail. The male is ornately patterned in rufous tones, gold, and blue gray, with pale spotting on the wings and back and dark spotting underneath. His head is an iridescent green-blue with a tufted crown; he has red facial skin and a white ring about the neck. The female is mottled brown above and plain below, without obvious head markings. Ring-necked Pheasants peck on the ground for seeds, grasses, and insects. Their vocalizations include a harsh *auk caw*, and they produce muffled wing fluttering. The adult male is illustrated.

Wild Turkey, *Meleagris gallopavo*
Family Phasianidae (Pheasants, Grouse, and Turkeys)
Size: 36–48"; males larger than females
Range: Throughout most of the contiguous United States
Habitat: Open mixed woodlands

The Wild Turkey is a very large, dark, ground-dwelling bird (but is slimmer than the domestic turkey). The head and neck appear small for the body size, and the legs are thick and stout. The heavily barred plumage is quite iridescent in strong light. The turkey's head and neck are covered with bluish, warty, crinkled bare skin that droops under the chin in a red wattle. Often foraging in flocks, Wild Turkeys search the ground for seeds, grubs, and insects, then roost at night in trees. Males emit the familiar *gobble*, while females are less vocal, making a soft *clucking* sound. In display the male hunches with his tail up and spread like a giant fan. The adult male is illustrated.

California Quail, *Callipepla californica*
Family Odontophoridae (Quail)
Size: 10"
Range: Pacific states, inland to Utah
Habitat: Open woodlands, shrubby areas, rural gardens
The California state bird, this is an elegant, gentle, little ground bird with a curious, forward-projecting head plume and a short curved bill. The male is grayish overall, with pale barring and scaling on the sides, flanks, and belly. The head is boldly marked with a rusty crown, black face, and white stripes above the eyes and around the chin. The female lacks the bold head pattern, and the plume is much smaller. California Quail travel in groups, picking the ground for seeds, insects, and berries. Their voice is a squawking, throaty, usually three-noted *caw-CAW-caw*, sometimes dubbed *chi-CA-go*. They roost low in trees or brush. The adult male is illustrated.

Pied-billed Grebe, *Podilymbus podiceps*
Family Podicipedidae (Grebes)
Size: 13"
Range: Throughout the contiguous United States
Habitat: Freshwater ponds and lakes

The Pied-billed Grebe is small and secretive. It lurks in sheltered waters, diving for small fish, leeches, snails, and crawfish. When alarmed, or to avoid predatory snakes and hawks, it sinks below the surface until only its head is above water. It is brownish overall but slightly darker above, with a tiny tail and short wings. Breeding adults have a conspicuous dark ring around the middle of the bill. The ring is missing in winter plumage. The grebe nests on a floating mat of vegetation. The breeding adult is illustrated.

Great Blue Heron, *Ardea herodias*
Family Ardeidae (Herons and Egrets)
Size: 46"
Range: Throughout the contiguous United States
Habitat: Most aquatic areas, including lakes, creeks, and marshes

The Great Blue Heron is the largest heron in North America. Walking slowly through shallow water or fields, it stalks fish, crabs, and small vertebrates, catching them with its massive bill. With long legs and a long neck, the heron is blue-gray overall, with a white face and a heavy yellow-orange bill. Its crown is black and supports plumes of medium length. The front of the neck is white, with distinct black chevrons fading into breast plumes. In flight the neck is tucked back, and the heron's wing beats are regular and labored. The adult is illustrated.

Cattle Egret, *Bubulcus ibis*
Family Ardeidae (Herons and Egrets)
Size: 20"
Range: Scattered regions throughout the United States, mostly in lower latitudes
Habitat: Upland fields, often near cattle in grazing land

The Cattle Egret is a widespread species originally from Africa and now quite common throughout much of North America. Unlike most herons, it is not normally found in aquatic environments. It forms groups around cattle, often perching atop them, and feeds on insects aroused by the movement of their hooves. It is stocky and all white with a comparatively short yellow bill and short black legs. In breeding plumage, the legs and bill turn a bright orange, and a peachy pale yellow forms on the crown, breast, and back. The illustration shows a nonbreeding adult.

Northern Harrier, *Circus cyaneus*
Family Accipitridae (Hawks and Eagles)
Size: 18"; females larger than males
Range: Throughout North America
Habitat: Open fields, wetlands

Also known as the Marsh Hawk, the Northern Harrier flies low over the landscape, methodically surveying its hunting grounds for rodents and other small animals. When it spots prey, aided by its acute hearing, it drops abruptly to the ground to attack. The Northern Harrier is a thin raptor with a long tail and long, flame-shaped wings that are broad in the middle. The face has a distinct owl-like facial disk, and there is a conspicuous white patch at the rump. Males are gray above, with a white, streaked breast and black wing tips. Females are brown with a barred breast. The juvenile is similar in plumage to the female, but with a pale belly. The female, below, and a male, above, are illustrated.

Sharp-shinned Hawk, *Accipiter striatus*
Family Accipitridae (Hawks and Eagles)
Size: 10–14"; females larger than males
Range: Throughout North America
Habitat: Woodlands, bushy areas, yards

The Sharp-shinned Hawk is North America's smallest accipiter, with a longish squared tail and stubby rounded wings. Its short wings allow for agile flight in tight, wooded quarters, where it quickly attacks small birds in flight. It is grayish above and light below, barred with pale rufous stripes. The eyes are set forward on the face to aid in the direct pursuit of prey. The juvenile is white below, streaked with brown. The Sharp-shinned Hawk may be confused with the larger Cooper's Hawk. The adult is illustrated.

Red-tailed Hawk, *Buteo jamaicensis*
Family Accipitridae (Hawks and Eagles)
Size: 20"
Range: Throughout North America
Habitat: Prairies, open country

This widespread species is the most common *buteo* (broad-winged hawks of the genus *Buteo*) in the United States. It has broad rounded wings and a stout hooked bill. Its plumage is highly variable depending on its geographic location. In general the underparts are light, with darker streaking that forms a dark band across the belly; the upperparts are dark brown; and the tail is rufous. Light spotting occurs along the scapulars. In flight there is a noticeable dark patch along the inner leading edge of the underwing. Red-tailed Hawks glide down from perches, such as telephone poles and posts in open country, to catch rodents. They also may hover to spot prey. They are usually seen alone or in pairs. The voice is the familiar *keeer*! The adult is illustrated.

American Kestrel, *Falco sparverius*
Family Falconidae (Falcons)
Size: 10"
Range: Throughout North America
Habitat: Open areas, roadsides, fences and telephone wires

North America's most common falcon, the American Kestrel is tiny (about the size of a robin), with long pointed wings and tail, and fast flight. It hovers above fields or dives from a perch in branches or on a wire to capture small animals and insects. The kestrel's upperparts are rufous and barred with black, its wings are blue gray, and its breast is buff or white and streaked with black spots. The head is patterned with a gray crown and vertical patches of black down the face. The female has rufous wings and a barred tail. Also known as the Sparrow Hawk, the Kestrel has a habit of flicking its tail up and down while perched. The adult male is illustrated.

American Coot, *Fulica americana*
Family Rallidae (Rails and Coots)
Size: 15"
Range: Throughout North America
Habitat: Wetlands, ponds, urban lawns and parks

The American Coot has a plump body and thick head and neck. A relatively tame bird, it is commonly seen in urban areas and parks. It dives for fish to feed, but it will also dabble like a duck or pick food from the ground. It is dark gray overall, with a black head and white bill that ends with a dark, narrow ring. The white trailing edge of the wings can be seen in flight. The toes are flanked with lobes that enable the coot to walk on water plants and swim efficiently. Juveniles are similar in plumage to adults but paler. Coots are often seen in very large flocks. The adult is illustrated.

Killdeer, *Charadrius vociferus*
Family Charadriidae (Plovers)
Size: 10"
Range: Throughout North America
Habitat: Fields, farmlands, lakeshores, meadows

The Killdeer gets its name from its piercing *kill-dee* call, which is often heard before these well-camouflaged plovers are seen. Well adapted to human-altered environments, the killdeer is quite widespread and gregarious. It has long pointed wings, a long tail, and a conspicuous double-banded breast. Its upper parts are dark brown, its belly is white, and its head is patterned with a white supercilium and forehead. The tail is rusty orange with a black tip. In flight a noticeable white stripe can be seen across the flight feathers. The Killdeer is known for its classic "broken wing" display, which it uses to distract predators from its nest and young. The adult is illustrated.

Rock Pigeon, *Columba livia*
Family Columbidae (Pigeons and Doves)
Size: 12"
Range: Throughout the contiguous United States
Habitat: Urban areas, farmland

Formerly known as the Rock Dove, the Rock Pigeon is the common pigeon seen in almost every urban area across the continent. Introduced from Europe, where it inhabits rocky cliffs, Rock Pigeons have adapted to city life, and domestication has resulted in a wide variety of plumage colors and patterns. The original, wild version is a stocky gray bird with a darker head and neck and green to purple iridescence along the sides of the neck. The eyes are bright red, and the bill has a fleshy white protuberance (cere) on the base of the upper mandible. There are two dark bars across the back when the wing is folded, the rump is white, and the tail has a dark terminal band. Variants range from white to brown to black, with many pattern combinations. The adult is illustrated.

Mourning Dove, *Zenaida macroura*
Family Columbidae (Pigeons and Doves)
Size: 12"
Range: Throughout the contiguous United States
Habitat: Open brushy areas, urban areas

The common Mourning Dove is a sleek, long-tailed dove with a thin neck, a small rounded head, and large black eyes. It is pale gray brown underneath and darker above, with some iridescence to the feathers on the neck. There are clear black spots on the tertials and some coverts and a dark spot on the upper neck below the eye. The pointed tail is edged with a white band. The Mourning Dove pecks on the ground for seeds and grains and walks with quick, short steps while bobbing its head. Its flight is strong and direct, and the wings create a whistle as the bird takes off. Its voice is a mournful, owl-like cooing. It is solitary or found in small groups but may form large flocks where food is abundant. The adult is illustrated.

Great Horned Owl, *Bubo virginianus*
Family Strigidae (Typical Owls)
Size: 22"
Range: Throughout North America
Habitat: Almost any environment, including forests, plains, and urban areas
Found throughout North America, the Great Horned Owl is large and strong, with an obvious facial disk and sharp, long talons. Plumage is variable: Eastern forms are brown overall with heavy barring, a rust-colored face, and a white chin patch, while western forms are grayer. The prominent ear tufts give the owl its name, and its eyes are large and yellow. The Great Horned Owl has exceptional hearing and sight. It feeds at night, perching on branches or posts and then swooping down on silent wings to catch birds, snakes, or mammals up to the size of a house cat. Its voice is a low *hoo-hoo-hoo*. The adult is illustrated.

Barn Owl, *Tyto alba*
Family Tytonidae (Barn Owl)
Size: 23"
Range: Throughout most of the contiguous United States except for the
northern Midwest regions
Habitat: Barns, farmland, open areas with mature trees
The Barn Owl is a large-headed pale owl with small dark eyes, a
heart-shaped facial disk, and long feathered legs. The wings, back,
tail, and crown are light rusty brown with light gray smudging and
small white dots. The underside, face, and underwing linings are
white, with spots of rust on the breast. Females are usually darker
than males, with more color and spotting across the breast and
sides. The facial disk is enclosed by a thin line of dark feathers. The
Barn Owl is a nocturnal hunter for rodents, and its call is a haunt-
ing, raspy *screeee*! The adult male is illustrated.

Eastern Screech-Owl, *Megascops asio*
Family Strigidae (Typical Owls)
Size: 8½"
Range: Central and eastern United States
Habitat: Wooded areas or parks, places where cavity-bearing trees exist

The Eastern Screech-Owl is a small, big-headed, eared owl with a short tail and bright yellow eyes. The highly camouflaged plumage ranges from reddish to brown to gray, depending on the region, but the red form is most common in the East. It is darker above, streaked and barred below. The ear tufts may be drawn back to give a rounded head appearance, and the bill is grayish green tipped with white. White spots on the margins of the coverts and scapulars create two white bars on the folded wing. The Eastern Screech-Owl is a nocturnal bird, hunting during the night for small mammals, insects, or fish. Its voice is a descending, whistling call or a rapid staccato of one pitch. The illustration shows a red morph adult. The similar Western Screech-Owl is found west of the Continental Divide.

Barred Owl, *Strix varia*
Family Strigidae (Typical Owls)
Size: 21"
Range: Eastern half of the United States, Pacific Northwest
Habitat: Wooded swamps, upland forests
The Barred Owl is a large, compact owl with a short tail and wings, rounded head, and big dark eyes. It lacks the ear tufts seen on the Great Horned Owl and has comparatively small talons. Its plumage is gray brown overall, with dark barring on the neck and breast, turning to streaking on the belly and flanks. It swoops from its perch to catch small rodents, frogs, or snakes. Its voice, often heard during the day, is a hooting *who-cooks-for-you* or a kind of bark. It nests in tree cavities vacated by other species. The illustration shows an adult.

Common Nighthawk, *Chordeiles minor*
Family Caprimulgidae (Nightjars and Nighthawks)
Size: 9"
Range: Throughout North America
Habitat: Variety of habitats: forests, marshes, plains, urban areas

The Common Nighthawk is primarily nocturnal but may often be seen flying during the day and evening hours, catching insects on the wing with bounding flight. It is cryptically mottled gray, brown, and black, with strong barring on an otherwise pale underside. A white breast band is evident in the male. The tail is long and slightly notched, and the wings are long and pointed, extending past the tail in the perched bird. In flight there is a distinct white patch on both sides of the wings. During the day the Common Nighthawk is usually seen roosting on posts or branches with its eyes closed. Its voice is a short, nasal buzzing sound. The adult male is illustrated.

Ruby-throated Hummingbird, *Archilochus colubris*
Family Trochilidae (Hummingbirds)
Size: 3½"
Range: Eastern half of the United States
Habitat: Areas with flowering plants, gardens, urban feeders

The Ruby-throated Hummingbird is a small, delicate bird able to hover on wings that beat at a blinding speed. It uses its long, needle-like bill to probe deep into flowers and lap up the nectar. Its feet are tiny and its body is white below and green above. Males have a dark green crown and iridescent red throat, or gorget. Females lack the colored gorget and have a light green crown and white-tipped tail feathers. Their behavior is typical of hummingbirds, hovering and buzzing from flower to flower, emitting chits and squeaks. Most of these birds migrate across the Gulf of Mexico to South America in the winter. The illustration shows an adult male (bottom) and female (top).

Calliope Hummingbird, *Stellula calliope*
Family Trochilidae (Hummingbirds)
Size: 3¼"
Range: West of the Continental Divide
Habitat: Brushy fields, feeders

The smallest breeding bird in North America, and an uncommon visitor to New England, the Calliope Hummingbird is a tiny, short-tailed and short-billed hummingbird with wings that extend beyond the tail when perched. The adult male is iridescent green above, on the head, and along the sides, while below it is white with an iridescent red, streaked gorget (sometimes held stiffly away from the body). Females are green above and buff below, with sparse, dark streaking on the throat. Although a tiny bird, the Calliope Hummingbird makes an arduous migration to wintering grounds in Mexico each year. It feeds on flower nectar or feeders from a hover or hunts small insects mid-air. Its voice is a quick, high-pitched *zip* and buzzy chatterings. The female (top) and male are illustrated.

Belted Kingfisher, *Megaceryle alcyon*
Family Alcedinidae (Kingfishers)
Size: 13"
Range: Throughout North America
Habitat: Creeks, lakes

The widespread but solitary Belted Kingfisher is stocky and has a large head with a long, powerful bill and a shaggy crest. It is grayish blue-green above and white below, with a thick blue band across its breast and white dotting on its back. White spots are at the lores. The female has an extra breast band of rufous hue, and is rufous along the flanks. Belted Kingfishers feed by springing from a perch along the water's edge or hovering above the water, then plunging headfirst to snatch fish, frogs, or tadpoles. Flight is uneven, and the kingfisher's vocalization is a raspy, rattling sound. The adult female is illustrated.

Downy Woodpecker, *Picoides pubescens*
Family Picidae (Woodpeckers)
Size: 6½"
Range: Throughout North America
Habitat: Woodlands, parks, urban areas, streamsides

The Downy Woodpecker is tiny, with a small bill and a relatively large head. It is white underneath with no barring and has black wings barred with white and a patch of white on its back. Its head is boldly patterned in white and black, and the male sports a red nape patch. The base of the bill joins the head with fluffy nasal tufts. Juveniles may show some red on the forehead and crown. The Downy Woodpecker forages for berries and insects in the bark and among the smaller twigs of trees. The very similar Hairy Woodpecker is larger, with a longer bill and more aggressive foraging behavior, sticking to larger branches and not clinging to twigs. The adult male is illustrated.

Hairy Woodpecker, *Picoides villosus*
Family Picidae (Woodpeckers)
Size: 9"
Range: Throughout North America
Habitat: Mixed woodlands, streamsides near large trees

The Hairy Woodpecker is very similar in plumage to the Downy Woodpecker but is larger and has a heavier bill. Also, it pecks for insects in tree bark or on larger branches and will not feed from smaller twigs, as does the Downy. It is mostly black above with a white patch on the back and outer tail feathers and some white spotting on the wings. The underside is white with no barring. The head is patterned black and white, and there are small nasal tufts. Males show a red patch on the back of the crown. Voice includes a high-pitched, squeaky *chip-chip*, as well as loud drumming. The adult female is illustrated.

Northern Flicker, *Colaptes auratus*
Family Picidae (Woodpeckers)
Size: 12½"
Range: Throughout North America
Habitat: Variety of habitats including suburbs and parks

The common Northern Flicker is a large, long-tailed wood-pecker often seen foraging on the ground for ants and other small insects. It is barred brown-and-black across the back, and is buff with black spotting below. Its head is brown, with a gray nape and crown. On the upper breast is a prominent half-circle of black, and the male has a red or black patch at the malar region (Eastern forms have a black malar area). Flight is undulating and shows an orange wing lining and white rump. The flicker's voice is a loud, sharp *keee,* and it will sometimes drum its bill repeatedly at objects, like a jackhammer. It is sometimes referred to as the red-shafted or yellow-shafted flicker. The adult Eastern race male is illustrated.

Say's Phoebe, *Sayornis saya*
Family Tyrannidae (Tyrant Flycatchers)
Size: 7½"
Range: Western and central United States
Habitat: Arid open country, shrub land

The Say's Phoebe is a fairly slim flycatcher with a long black tail. It is pale gray brown above, with lighter wings bars. The underside is whitish to gray under the chin and breast, fading to orange-brown on the belly and undertail coverts. Its head has a flat crown that often peaks toward the rear, and the bird has dark eyes, lores, and bill. It fly-catches for insects from a perch on rocks or twigs. The Say's Phoebe voices a high, whistled *pit-eur*, and often pumps or flares out its tail. The adult is illustrated.

Western Kingbird, *Tyrannus verticalis*
Family Tyrannidae (Tyrant Flycatchers)
Size: 8¾"
Range: Mostly in central and western United States, but found farther east as well
Habitat: Open fields, agricultural areas

The Western Kingbird is a relatively slender flycatcher, with a stout black bill and a slightly rounded, black tail with white along the outer edge. It is grayish or greenish-brown above, pale gray on the breast, and bright yellow on the belly, sides, and undertail coverts. The head is light gray, with a white throat and malar area, and dark gray at the lores and behind the eye. It has a small, reddish crown patch that is normally concealed. Western Kingbirds fly-catch for insects from perches on branches, posts, or wires, and the voice is composed of quick, high-pitched zips and chits. The adult is illustrated.

Blue Jay, *Cyanocitta cristata*
Family Corvidae (Jays, Magpies, and Crows)
Size: 11"
Range: East of the Continental Divide
Habitat: Woodlands, rural and urban areas

The solitary Blue Jay is sturdy and crested. It is bright blue above and white below, with a thick, tapered black bill. There is a white patch around the eye that extends to the chin, bordered by a thin, black "necklace" extending to the nape. The blue jay has a conspicuous white wing bar and dark barring on the wings and tail. In flight the white outer edges of the tail are visible. The jay alternates shallow wing beats with glides. Omnivorous, the Blue Jay eats just about anything, but especially consumes acorns, nuts, fruits, insects, and small vertebrates. It is a raucous and noisy bird, and quite bold. Sometimes it mimics the calls of birds of prey. The adult is illustrated.

Western Scrub Jay, *Aphelocoma californica*
Family Corvidae (Jays, Magpies, and Crows)
Size: 11½"
Range: Western United States
Habitat: Open areas of scrub oak, urban areas

The Western Scrub Jay is long-necked, sleek, and crestless. Its upperparts are deep blue, with a distinct, lighter gray-brown mantle. Its underparts are pale gray, becoming white on the belly and undertail coverts. It has a thin white superciliary stripe, the malar area is dark gray, and the throat is streaked with white and gray above a dull gray "necklace" across the breast. The bird's flight is an undulating combination of rapid wing beats and swooping glides. Its diet consists of nuts, seeds, insects, and fruit. The adult is illustrated.

Black-billed Magpie, *Pica hudsonia*
Family Corvidae (Jays, Magpies, and Crows)
Size: 19"
Range: Western United States up to Alaska
Habitat: Riparian areas, open woodlands, pastures, rural areas

The Black-billed Magpie is heavy, with broad wings and an extremely long, graduated tail. It has striking pied plumage: black on the head, upper breast, and back; dark, iridescent green-blue on the wings and tail; and crisp white on the scapulars and belly. Its legs are dark and stout, and its bill is thick at the base. Juvenile birds have a much shorter tail. Magpies travel in small groups and are opportunistic feeders, eating insects, nuts, eggs, or carrion. The voice is a whining, questioning *mag?* or a harsh *wok-wok*. The adult is illustrated.

American Crow, *Corvus brachyrhynchos*
Family Corvidae (Jays, Magpies, and Crows)
Size: 17½"
Range: Throughout the contiguous United States
Habitat: Open woodlands, pastures, rural fields, dumps

The American Crow is widespread, found across the continent. Known for its familiar, loud, grating *caw, caw* vocalization, the crow is a large, stocky bird with a short rounded tail, broad wings, and a thick, powerful bill. Plumage is glistening black overall in all stages of development. It will eat almost anything and often forms loose flocks with other crows. The adult is illustrated.

Common Raven, *Corvus corax*
Family Corvidae (Jays, Magpies, and Crows)
Size: 24"
Range: Western and northern United States to Alaska, including the Appalachian Mountains
Habitat: Wide range of habitats, including deserts, mountains, canyons, forests

The Common Raven is a large, stocky, gruff corvid with a long, massive bill that slopes directly into the forehead. The wings are narrow and long, and the tail is rounded or wedge shaped. The entire body is glossy black, sometimes bluish, and the neck is laced with pointed, shaggy feathers. Quite omnivorous, the Common Raven feeds on carrion, refuse, insects, and roadkill. It has a varied voice that includes deep croaking. Ravens may soar and engage in rather acrobatic flight. Crows are similar but are smaller, with proportionately smaller bills. The adult is illustrated.

Barn Swallow, *Hirundo rustica*
Family Hirundinidae (Swallows)
Size: 6½"
Range: Throughout the contiguous United States
Habitat: Old buildings, caves, open rural areas near bridges

Widespread and common, the Barn Swallow has narrow, pointed wings and a long, deeply forked tail. It is pale below and dark blue above, with a rusty orange forehead and throat. In males the underparts are pale orange, while females are a pale cream color below. Barn Swallows are graceful, fluid fliers, and they often forage in groups to catch insects in flight. The voice is a loud, repetitive chirping or clicking. They build cup-shaped nests of mud on almost any protected man-made structure. The adult male is illustrated.

70

Black-capped Chickadee, *Poecile atricapillus*
Family Paridae (Chickadees and Titmice)
Size: 5¼"
Range: Northern latitudes across the United States, Alaska
Habitat: Mixed woodlands, rural gardens, feeders
The Black-capped Chickadee is small, compact, and active, with short, rounded wings and a tiny black bill. It is gray above and lighter gray or dusky below, with a contrasting black cap and throat patch. It is quite similar to the Eastern Carolina Chickadee, which occurs in the Southeast. Its voice sounds like its name— *chick-a-dee-dee-dee*—or is a soft *fee-bay*. The chickadee is quite social and feeds on a variety of seeds, berries, and insects found in trees and shrubs. The adult is illustrated.

White-breasted Nuthatch, *Sitta carolinensis*
Family Sittidae (Nuthatches)
Size: 5¾"
Range: Throughout the contiguous United States
Habitat: Mixed oak or coniferous woodlands
The White-breasted Nuthatch has a large head; a wide neck; short, rounded wings; and a short tail. It is blue gray above and pale gray below, with rusty smudging on the lower flanks and undertail coverts. The breast and face are white, and a black crown merges with the mantle. The bill is long, thin, and upturned at the tip. To forage, the White-breasted Nuthatch creeps headfirst down tree trunks to pick out insects and seeds. Its voice is a nasal, repetitive *auk, auk, auk*. It nests in tree cavities high off the ground. The adult male is illustrated.

House Wren, *Troglodytes aedon*
Family Troglodytidae (Wrens)
Size: 4¾"
Range: Throughout the contiguous United States
Habitat: Shrubby areas, rural gardens
The House Wren is a loud, drab wren with short, rounded wings
and a thin, pointed, downcurved bill. Plumage is brown and barred
above and pale gray brown below, with barring on the lower belly,
undertail coverts, and tail. The head is lighter on the throat, at
the lores, and above the eyes. House Wrens feed in the brush for
insects and sing rapid, melodic, chirping songs, often while cock-
ing their tails downward. The adult is illustrated.

Ruby-crowned Kinglet, *Regulus calendula*
Family Regulidae (Kinglets)
Size: 4"
Range: Throughout North America
Habitat: Shrubs and leafy trees

The Ruby-crowned Kinglet is a tiny, plump songbird with a short tail and a diminutive, thin bill. It has a habit of nervously twitching its wings as it actively flits through vegetation, gleaning small insects and larvae. It may also hover in search of food. Plumage is pale olive green above and paler below, with patterned wings and pale wing bars on the upper coverts. There are white eye rings or crescents around the eyes. The bright red crest of the male bird is faintly noticeable unless the crest is raised. Its voice is a very high-pitched whistling *seeee*. The adult is illustrated.

American Robin, *Turdus migratorius*
Family Turdidae (Thrushes)
Size: 10"
Range: Throughout North America
Habitat: Widespread in a variety of habitats, including woodlands, fields, parks, lawns

Familiar and friendly, the American Robin is a large thrush with long legs and a long tail. It commonly holds its head cocked and keeps its wing tips lowered beneath its tail. It is gray brown above and rufous below, with a darker head and contrasting white eye crescents and loral patches. The chin is streaked black and white, and the bill is yellow with darker edges. Females are typically paler overall, and the juvenile shows spots of white above and dark spots below. Robins forage on the ground for earthworms and insects and in trees for berries. The robin's song is a series of high, musical phrases, sounding like *cheery, cheer-u-up, cheerio*. The adult male is illustrated.

Gray Catbird, *Dumetella carolinensis*
Family Mimidae (Mockingbirds, Catbirds, and Thrashers)
Size: 8½"
Range: Throughout the contiguous United States; less common in the far West
Habitat: Understory of woodland edges, shrubs, rural gardens
The solitary Gray Catbird is sleek and has a long neck and sturdy pointed bill. It is uniformly gray except for its rufous undertail coverts, black crown, and black, rounded tail. It is quite secretive and spends most of its time hidden in thickets close to the ground, picking through the substrate for insects, berries, and seeds. Its call includes a nasal catlike *meew*, from which its name is derived, although it will also mimic the songs of other birds. To escape danger, the Gray Catbird will often choose to run away rather than fly. The adult is illustrated.

Northern Mockingbird, *Mimus polyglottos*
Family Mimidae (Mockingbirds, Catbirds, and Thrashers)
Size: 10½"
Range: Lower latitudes across the United States, up to New England
Habitat: Open fields, grassy areas near vegetative cover, suburbs, parks

The Northern Mockingbird is constantly vocalizing. Its scientific name, *polyglottos*, means "many voices," alluding to its amazing mimicry of the songs of other birds. Sleek, long-tailed, and long-legged, it shows gray plumage above with darker wings and tail and off-white to brownish gray plumage below. The bird has two white wing bars; short, dark eye stripes; and pale eye rings. In flight, it reveals conspicuous white patches on the inner primaries and coverts and white outer tail feathers. Like other mimids, the mockingbird forages on the ground for insects and berries, intermittently flicking its wings. The adult is illustrated.

Brown Thrasher, *Toxostoma rufum*
Family Mimidae (Mockingbirds, Catbirds, and Thrashers)
Size: 11"
Range: East of the Continental Divide
Habitat: Woodlands, thickets, urban gardens, orchards

The Brown Thrasher is primarily a ground-dwelling bird that thrashes through leaves and dirt for insects and plant material. It has a long tail and legs and a medium length, slightly decurved bill. Its plumage is rufous brown above, including the tail, and whitish below, and is heavily streaked with brown or black. There are two prominent, pale wing bars and pale outermost corners to the tail. Its eyes are yellow to orange. Its voice is a variety of musical phrases, often sung from a conspicuous perch. The illustration shows an adult.

European Starling, *Sturnus vulgaris*
Family Sturnidae (Starlings)
Size: 8½"
Range: Throughout the contiguous United States
Habitat: Found almost anywhere, particularly in rural fields, gardens, dumps, urban parks

Introduced from Europe, the European Starling has successfully infiltrated most habitats in North America and competes with native birds for nest cavities. It is a stocky, sturdy, aggressive bird that is glossy black overall with a sheen of green or purple. The breeding adult has a yellow bill and greater iridescence, while the adult in winter is more flat black, with a black bill and numerous white spots. The tail is short and square. Starlings form very large, compact flocks and fly directly on pointed, triangular wings. Its diet is highly variable and includes insects, grains, and berries. Vocalizations include loud, wheezy whistles and clucks and imitations of other birdsongs. The breeding adult is illustrated.

Cedar Waxwing, *Bombycilla cedrorum*
Family Bombycillidae (Waxwings)
Size: 7"
Range: Throughout the contiguous United States
Habitat: Woodlands, swamps, urban areas near berry trees
Quite similar to the Bohemian Waxwing, the Cedar Waxwing is a compact, crested songbird with pointed wings and a short tail. The sleek, smooth plumage is brownish gray overall with paler underparts, a yellowish wash on the belly, and white undertail coverts. The head pattern is striking, with a crisp black mask thinly bordered by white. The tail is tipped with bright yellow, and the tips of the secondary feathers are coated with a unique red, waxy substance. Cedar Waxwings will form large flocks and devour berries from a tree, then move on to the next. They may also catch small insects while in flight. Their voice is an extremely high-pitched, whistling *seee*. The adult is illustrated.

Yellow-rumped Warbler, *Dendroica coronata*
Family Parulidae (Wood Warblers)
Size: 5½"
Range: Throughout North America
Habitat: Deciduous and coniferous woodlands, suburbs with wax myrtle

Two races of this species occur in North America. The "myrtle" form is dispersed across North America, and the "Audubon's" form is seen west of the Rockies. The myrtle variety is blue-gray above, with dark streaks, and white below, with black streaking below the chin and a bright yellow side patch. There is a black mask across the face, bordered by a thin superciliary stripe above and a white throat below. The nonbreeding adult males and females are paler, with a more brownish cast to the upperparts. The long-ish tail has white spots on either side and meets with the conspicuous yellow rump. The Audubon's variety has a yellow chin and gray face. Yellow-rumped Warblers prefer to eat berries and insects. The adult male myrtle form is illustrated.

Spotted Towhee, *Pipilo maculatus*
Family Emberizidae (Sparrows and Buntings)
Size: 8½"
Range: Western half of the United States
Habitat: Thickets, suburban shrubs, gardens

The Spotted Towhee is a large, long-tailed sparrow with a thick, short bill and sturdy legs. It forages on the ground in dense cover by kicking back both feet at once to uncover insects, seeds, and worms. It is black above, including the head and upper breast, and has rufous sides and a white belly. It has white wing bars, white spotting on its scapulars and mantle, and white corners on its tail. The eye color is red. Females are like the males, but are brown above. The Spotted Towhee was once conspecific with the Eastern Towhee, known as the rufous-sided towhee. The adult male is illustrated.

Song Sparrow, *Melospiza melodia*
Family Emberizidae (Sparrows and Buntings)
Size: 6"
Range: Throughout North America
Habitat: Thickets, shrubs, woodland edges near water

One of the most common sparrows, the Song Sparrow is fairly plump, with a long, rounded tail. It is brown and gray with streaking above and white below, with heavy dark or brownish streaking that often congeals into a discreet spot in the middle of its breast. Its head has a dark crown with a gray medial stripe, dark eye lines, and a dark malar stripe above the white chin. Song Sparrows are usually seen in small groups or individually, foraging on the ground for insects and seeds. The song is a series of chips and trills of variable pitch, and the call is a *chip, chip, chip*. The adult is illustrated.

White-crowned Sparrow, *Zonotrichia leucophrys*
Family Emberizidae (Sparrows and Buntings)
Size: 7"
Range: Throughout North America
Habitat: Brushy areas, woodland edges, gardens

The White-crowned Sparrow has a rounded head, sometimes with a raised peak, and a fairly long, slightly notched tail. It is brownish above, streaked on the mantle, and shows pale wing bars. The underside is grayish on the breast, fading to pale brown on the belly and flanks. The head is gray below the eyes and boldly patterned black and white above the eyes, with a white medial crown stripe. The bill is bright yellow orange. White-crowned Sparrows forage on the ground, often in loose flocks, scratching for insects, seeds, and berries. Their song is variable, but it usually starts with one longer whistle, followed by several faster notes. The adult is illustrated.

Dark-eyed Junco, *Junco hyemalis*
Family Emberizidae (Sparrows and Buntings)
Size: 6½"
Range: Throughout North America
Habitat: Thickets, rural gardens, open coniferous or mixed woodlands

The Dark-eyed Junco is a small, plump sparrow with a short, conical, pink bill and several distinct variations in plumage. One of the more common races is the "Oregon" junco, with its rusty brown mantle, sides, and flanks; white belly; and black head and breast. Sexes are similar, but the female is paler overall. The white outer tail feathers are obvious in flight. Juncos hop about on the ground, often in groups, picking up insects and seeds. The voice is a staccato, monotone chirping trill. Also common is the Gray-headed Junco, which is pale gray overall, with a rufous mantle. The adult male of the Oregon race is illustrated.

Scarlet Tanager, *Piranga olivacea*
Family Cardinalidae (Cardinals, Grosbeaks, Tanagers, and Buntings)
Size: 7"
Range: Eastern half of the United States
Habitat: Leafy deciduous forests, suburban parks

The Scarlet Tanager is a secretive bird of the high canopy that is often detected first by its voice, despite its bright plumage. The breeding male is rich scarlet red overall, with contrasting black wings and tail. Females and nonbreeding males are similar, colored olive-yellow above and yellow below, with dark wings and tail. Males in fall molt show a patchwork of yellow, green, and red feathers. Scarlet Tanagers feed on insects, spiders, and berries at the upper levels of large trees, and they sing a series of raspy, quick phrases, comparable to that of a robin. The breeding (bottom) and nonbreeding (top) males are illustrated.

Northern Cardinal, *Cardinalis cardinalis*
Family Cardinalidae (Cardinals, Grosbeaks, Tanagers, and Buntings)
Size: 8½"
Season: Eastern and central United States to Arizona
Habitat: Woodlands with thickets, suburban gardens
The Northern Cardinal with its thick, powerful bill eats mostly seeds but will also forage for fruit and insects. It is often found in pairs and is quite common at suburban feeders. It is a long-tailed songbird with a thick, short, orange bill and tall crest. The male is red overall with a black mask and chin. The female is brownish above, dusky below, and crested and has a dark front to its face. Juveniles are similar to the female but have a black bill. The voice is a musical *weeta-weeta* or *woit* heard from a tall, exposed perch. The illustration shows an adult male (bottom) and female (top).

Red-winged Blackbird, *Agelaius phoeniceus*
Family Icteridae (Blackbirds, Orioles, and Grackles)
Size: 8½"
Range: Throughout North America
Habitat: Marshes, meadows, agricultural areas near water

The Red-winged Blackbird is a widespread, ubiquitous, chunky meadow dweller that forms huge flocks during the nonbreeding season. The male is deep black overall, with bright orange-red lesser coverts and pale medial coverts that form an obvious shoulder patch in flight, but may be partially concealed on the perched bird. The female is barred in tan and dark brown overall, with pale superciliary stripes and a pale malar patch. The blackbirds forage marshlands for insects, spiders, and seeds. The voice is a loud, raspy, vibrating *konk-a-leee* given from a perch atop a tall reed or branch. The male (below) and female (above) are illustrated.

Brewer's Blackbird, *Euphagus cyanocephalus*
Family Icteridae (Blackbirds, Orioles, and Grackles)
Size: 9"
Range: Throughout the contiguous United States; most common farther west
Habitat: Meadows, pastures, open woodlands, urban areas
The Brewer's Blackbird is small headed and dark, with a short bill and bright yellow eyes (in males). The breeding male is glossy black overall, with purple iridescence on the head and breast and green iridescence on the wings and tail. During winter the plumage is not as glossy. Females are drab brownish overall and usually have dark eyes. Brewer's Blackbirds forage on the ground for seeds and insects, often while bowed over with their tails sticking up. The voice is a short, coarse *zhet*, and a longer, creaky trill. These blackbirds form large flocks in winter, along with other blackbird species. The breeding adult male is illustrated.

Common Grackle, *Quiscalus quiscula*
Family Icteridae (Blackbirds, Orioles, and Grackles)
Size: 12½"
Range: Eastern half of the United States
Habitat: Pastures, open woodlands, urban parks

The Common Grackle is a large blackbird with an elongate body; a long, heavy bill; and long tail, which is fatter toward the tip and is often folded into a keel shape. Plumage is overall black with a metallic sheen of purple on the head and brown on the wings and underside. The eyes are a contrasting light yellow color. Quite social, grackles form huge flocks with other blackbirds and forage on the ground for just about any kind of food, including insects, grains, refuse, and crustaceans. Their voice is a high-pitched, rasping trill. The illustration shows an adult male.

Purple Finch, *Carpodacus purpureus*
Family Fringillidae (Finches)
Size: 6"
Range: Eastern half of the United States; Pacific states
Habitat: Open coniferous and mixed woodlands, rural gardens and parks

The Purple Finch is a sturdy, large-headed finch with a short notched tail and a thick conical bill. The male is brownish red above with brown streaking and whitish below with dusky or pink streaking. The head and breast are not purple, but rosy red, and there is pale feathering at the base of the bill. Females and juveniles are brownish and heavily streaked, with noticeably darker facial markings on the crown, auricular, and malar regions. Purple Finches forage in small groups in trees or on the ground for seeds and insects. Their voice is a long, jumbled song of high whistles, cheeps, and trills. The adult female (top) and adult male are illustrated.

House Finch, *Carpodacus mexicanus*
Family Fringillidae (Finches)
Size: 6"
Range: Throughout the contiguous United States
Habitat: Woodland edges, urban areas

The House Finch is a western species that was introduced to eastern North America and is now common and widespread across the country. It is a relatively slim finch, with a longish, slightly notched tail and a short conical bill with a downcurved culmen. The male is brown above with streaking on the back, while below it is pale with heavy streaking. An orange-red wash pervades the supercilium, throat, and upper breast. The female is a drab gray brown, with similar streaking on the back and underside and no red on the face or breast. House Finches have a variable diet that includes seeds, insects, and fruit, and they are often the most abundant birds at feeders. Their voice is a rapid musical warble. The adult male is illustrated.

Evening Grosbeak, *Coccothraustes vespertinus*
Family Fringillidae (Finches)
Size: 8"
Range: Northern and mountainous regions of the United States; Pacific Northwest
Habitat: Coniferous or mixed woodlands, rural gardens

The Evening Grosbeak is a comical-looking finch with a large head, short stubby tail, and enormous conical bill. In the male, plumage fades from dark brown on the head to bright yellow toward the rump and belly. His wings are black, with large white patches on the secondaries and tertials. The yellow superciliums merge with his flat forehead and meet his pale yellow-green bill. The legs are short and pinkish. Females are grayish overall, with choppy white markings on the wings. Evening Grosbeaks travel in flocks to feed on seeds and berries in the upper canopy and will often visit feeders, preferring sunflower seeds. Their voice is a series of short, spaced, rattling *cheep* notes. The male (bottom) and female (top) are illustrated.

Pine Siskin, *Carduelis pinus*
Family Fringillidae (Finches)
Size: 5"
Range: Throughout the contiguous United States; Alaska
Habitat: Coniferous woodlands, rural gardens

The Pine Siskin is a small, cryptically colored finch with a short tail and narrow, pointed bill. The male's head and back are light brown overall, heavily streaked with darker brown. His underside is whitish and streaked in darker shades. There is a prominent yellow wing bar on the greater coverts and yellow on the flight feather edges and at the base of the primaries. Females are marked similarly, with a darker underside and white—not yellow—wing bars. Individuals can be quite variable as to the amount of streaking and the prominence of the yellow coloring. Pine Siskins forage energetically in small groups for seeds and insects, sometimes clinging upside down on twigs to reach food. Their voice consists of high-pitched, erratic, raspy chips and trills. The adult male is illustrated.

American Goldfinch, *Spinus tristis*
Family Fringillidae (Finches)
Size: 5"
Range: Throughout the contiguous United States
Habitat: Open fields, marshes, urban feeders

The American Goldfinch is a small, cheerful, social finch with a short, notched tail and a small conical bill. In winter it is brownish gray, lighter underneath, with black wings and tail. There are two white wing bars and bright yellow on the shoulders, around the eyes, and along the chin. In breeding plumage, the male becomes light yellow across the back, underside, and head; develops a black forehead and loral area; and the bill becomes orange. Females look similar to the winter males. American Goldfinches forage by actively searching for insects and seeds of all kinds, particularly thistle seeds. Their voice is a meandering, musical warble that includes high *cheep* notes. The breeding female (top) and breeding male (bottom) are illustrated.

House Sparrow, *Passer domesticus*
Family Passeridae (Old World Sparrows)
Size: 6¼"
Range: Throughout the contiguous United States
Habitat: Urban environments, rural pastures
Introduced from Europe, the House Sparrow is ubiquitous in almost every city in the United States and is often the only sparrow-type bird seen in urban areas. It is stocky, aggressive, and gregarious and has a relatively large head and a short finch-like bill. Males are streaked brown and black above and are pale below. The lores, chin, and breast are black, while the crown and auriculars are gray. There are prominent white wing bars at the median coverts. In winter the male lacks the dark breast patch. Females are drab overall, with a lighter bill and pale supercilium. House Sparrows have a highly varied diet, including grains, insects, berries, and crumbs from the local cafe. Their voice is a series of rather unmusical chirps. The breeding female (top) and breeding male (bottom) are illustrated.

REPTILES

Eastern Fence Lizard, *Sceloporus undulatus*
Family Phrynosomatidae (Iguanid Lizards)
Size: Up to 6"
Range: Southern Rocky Mountains to the Atlantic coast
Habitat: A wide variety of sunny habitats, including grasslands, woodlands, brushy areas

The Eastern Fence Lizard includes several subspecies of varying color patterns, including grayish or brownish, with longitudinal striping, spotting, or a combination of the two. These common lizards are sometimes called blue-bellies because the males show blue patches on the belly and chin. The Eastern Fence Lizard is compact and has a long tail, big feet, a blunt face, and scaled, dry skin. Solitary and active during the day, these lizards scurry through sheltered areas or among trees, feeding on all kinds of insects and other invertebrates. The similar Western Fence Lizard lives in the far western United States.

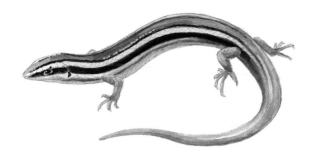

Western Skink, *Eumeces skiltonianus*

Family Scincidae (Skinks)
Size: Up to 9", including tail
Range: West of the Rocky Mountains
Habitat: A wide variety of habitats, including woodlands, streamsides, fields

Like the other skinks, the Western Skink has a long, narrow, cylindrical body; a long tapering tail; small limbs; and smooth, shiny scales. It is distinctively colored with a broad brown stripe down its back, blackish stripes along its sides, and pale stripes between these. The tail is bright blue in juveniles, becoming grayish in mature individuals. Breeding males develop orange markings under the chin and on the belly. Active during the day, Western Skinks usually stay hidden under leaves, rocks, or stumps. They feed on insects, spiders, sow bugs, earthworms, and other invertebrates. They also dig burrows and remain in them for winter in cold climates.

Green Anole, *Anolis carolinensis*
Family Iguanidae (Iguanid Lizards)
Size: Up to 8" long
Range: Southeastern United States
Habitat: Virtually any habitat with trees, vines, or tall brush, including buildings and fences in urban areas

The Green Anole is a common, arboreal lizard that is often raised as a pet. It has a thin body, a long tail, a pointed snout, and padded toes to aid in climbing vertical surfaces. Its color can vary from bright green to brown or gray, depending on environmental factors or stress, but the undersides are always paler. Males develop an extendable, pinkish skin flap under the throat (the "throat fan"). Active during the day, Green Anoles often bask head down on tree branches, buildings, or fences. They forage with stealth and patience for their prey of insects and other invertebrates.

Northern Alligator Lizard, *Elgaria coerulea*

Family Anguidae (Glass and Alligator Lizards)

Size: Up to 12" long

Range: Pacific Northwest to coastal California and the Sierra Nevada

Habitat: Cool and moist woodlands or fields

The Northern Alligator Lizard has a stout body, a triangular head with a long snout, short limbs, and distinct grooves along each side of its body, allowing it to expand for breathing and feeding. The skin is greenish brown to bluish, with variable dark spots that may coalesce into bands or stripes. The belly is paler, with thin dark stripes that run between the scales. Juveniles are very smooth (like a skink), with a wide light stripe down the back and no dark bands. Northern Alligator Lizards are secretive, moving through and under logs, rocks, and dense brush in search of insects, eggs, or small vertebrates. If captured, the lizard may detach its tail or emit feces.

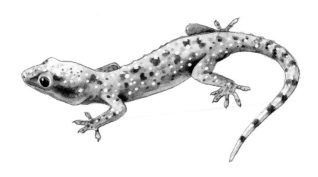

Mediterranean House Gecko, *Hemidactylus turcicus*
Family Gekkonidae (Geckos)
Size: Up to 5" long
Range: Throughout southeastern United States
Habitat: Developed areas, walls of buildings, trees; lights at night
The Mediterranean House Gecko is a species native to the Mediterranean region that has been introduced to the southern United States and maintains a stable or growing population. It has a large head with a rounded snout, eyes that are lidless and have vertical pupils, and feet with adhesive pads to aid in climbing vertical surfaces. The skin color can range from pale gray to brownish or tan with dark spots (colors are usually palest at night). The body is covered with rough, whitish bumps. Most active at night, Mediterranean House Geckos feed on moths and other insects by waiting quietly, then snatching up prey as it draws near. They make a high-pitched squeak or chirp, somewhat like a mouse or small bird.

Racer, *Coluber constrictor*
Family Colubridae (Colubrid Snakes)
Size: Up to 60"
Range: Throughout the contiguous United States
Habitat: Brush and thickets, often near water; in suburbs

With nearly a dozen subspecies, each with a different coloration, the Racer is often sighted in residential areas. It is a long, thin, speedy snake. Its eyes are dark and relatively large, its neck is thin, and its scales are smooth. The Racer's color can be black, dark gray, bluish green, or brownish above, paler below, often with a whitish throat area. Young snakes are paler overall, with rounded, brownish spots along its back. Burrowing during the night, they are most active in the daytime, foraging on the ground for insects or small vertebrates. They are capable of climbing trees to escape danger. Although not poisonous, they are capable of inflicting painful bites. The Black Racer is illustrated.

Milk Snake, *Lampropeltis triangulum*
Family Colubridae (Colubrid Snakes)
Size: Up to 60"
Range: East of the Rocky Mountains
Habitat: Highly variable depending on region; forests, fields, wetlands, streamsides, farmland

One of the most widespread snakes in the United States, the Milk Snake has a narrow body, a small head, and smooth scales. There is much geographical variation in color and pattern, but black-bordered, reddish or brown bands or blotches appear over a yellowish, tan, or pale gray background. The lighter background color is widest toward the base. In many cases there is a V-shaped mark on the top of the head, and the belly may have a distinct black-and-white pattern. Active day or night, favoring covered areas under logs or in rocks, Milk Snakes prey on small mammals, eggs, and other reptiles, subduing them by constriction and suffocation. This snake's common name is derived from the myth that it sucks the milk of cows.

Corn Snake, *Elaphe guttata*
Family Colubridae (Colubrid Snakes)
Size: Up to 72"
Range: Southeastern and south central United States
Habitat: Quite variable; streamsides, woodlands, rocky slopes, farmlands
Also known as the Red Rat Snake, the Corn Snake is handsome, has a long body and docile disposition, and is popular in the pet trade. Eastern individuals are brownish yellow, with dark-bordered, orange, or reddish saddle-like marks down the back and smaller marks along the sides. Farther west, the background color is more grayish, with brown marks. In all varieties the underside is paler with dark speckles, and the top of the head usually sports a pointed mark between the eyes. Staying in burrows, crevices, or under rocks at night, Corn Snakes are active during the daytime, searching for small mammals, birds, bats, and reptiles, which they subdue by constriction. Their common name is derived from the fact that these snakes are found near corn storage areas, attracted to the rodents that feed there.

Gopher Snake, *Pituophis catenifer*
Family Colubridae (Colubrid Snakes)
Size: 48"–96"
Range: Western and central United States
Habitat: Desert, pine-oak woodlands, rocky areas, scrubland, prairies

The Gopher Snake is widespread, large, and powerful. It has more than a dozen subspecies and goes by many common names, including pine snake, pine-gopher, and bull snake. Its body is thick, with ridged scales on the upper surface, and the eyes have round pupils. The base color is light brown, pale gray, or yellowish, heavily marked with reddish-brown or blackish blotches and spots. Some varieties are nearly solid black; others have distinct, lengthwise stripes. Chiefly active during the day, Gopher Snakes hide in rodent or tortoise burrows, crevices, or under rocks during the day but often can be seen at night in warm weather. They hunt on the ground, in trees, or in burrows for rodents and other reptiles, lunging at prey and constricting it with their strong bodies. If confronted, the gopher snake will flatten its head, hiss, and quiver its tail.

Common Garter Snake, *Thamnophis sirtalis*
Family Colubridae (Colubrid Snakes)
Size: Up to 40"
Range: Throughout the contiguous United States
Habitat: Well-vegetated areas near water, marshes, urban parks

The Common Garter Snake is, true to its name, widespread and common, with more than ten subspecies that commonly frequent developed areas and home gardens. It is a thin, medium-size snake with a head slightly wider than its body and relatively large eyes. The skin has keeled scales and is extremely variable in color, depending on subspecies, but always shows three longitudinal stripes—one running across the top of the back and two along the sides. Often there are blackish spots between the stripes. The underparts are pale. Common Garter Snakes freely move from land to water. They feed on insects, aquatic invertebrates, fish, and small mammals. They are relatively harmless but can bite and may emit foul-smelling fluid if trapped.

Eastern Coral Snake, *Micrurus fulvius*
Family Elapidae (Elapid Snakes)
Size: Up to 24" or longer
Range: Southeastern United States
Habitat: Woodlands near water, rural gardens, hammocks

The Eastern Coral Snake is generally secretive in nature, but caution is advised, as its bite is venomous and can be fatal. Its body is slender, with smooth, shiny scales and a small, blunt-tipped head (the head is no wider than the body). The color is striking, with wide red and black bands separated by thinner yellow bands. The head is black, with a wide yellow band just behind the eyes. Many harmless snakes have similar colors, but the Eastern Coral Snake has one distinguishing mark: The red and yellow bands are always adjacent to one another. Eastern Coral Snakes move through dense leaf litter and fallen wood, feeding on smaller snakes, other reptiles, and amphibians.

Western Rattlesnake, *Crotalus viridis*
Family Viperidae (Pit Vipers)
Size: Up to 62"
Range: Western United States
Habitat: Quite variable depending on region: forests, sand dunes, grasslands, rocky areas up to timberline

The Western Rattlesnake is a thick, rough-scaled, venomous pit viper with a flat, wide, triangular head, retractable fangs, and a tail tipped with horny segments that buzz when shaken. This species comprises several subspecies with variable colorations and sizes. The background color can be pale yellow, brown, reddish, greenish, or dark gray, with darker, light-edged blotches along the back that merge to cross bands on the tail. There is usually a pale stripe extending from the eye to the corner of the mouth. Western Rattlesnakes are active most of the day, except in very hot weather, when they retreat into burrows made by mammals. They feed on small mammals, reptiles, and amphibians, striking and biting the prey, letting the venom kill the victim, and then ingesting it. Much caution is advised around these snakes: Although they usually avoid humans, if surprised they can inflict a painful or lethal bite.

Pond Slider, *Chrysemys scripta*
Family Emydidae (Pond and Box Turtles)
Size: Up to 11" long (carapace)
Range: Southeastern United States; Texas to West Virginia
Habitat: Slow-moving streams and rivers, lakes and ponds with muddy bottoms

The Pond Slider is a common and gregarious pond turtle with a relatively flat carapace, webbed feet, and an unhinged plastron. Three distinct subspecies exist, all with greenish-yellow and dark green or black stripes or reticulations on the scutes and bright yellow, orange, or red markings behind the eyes. The familiar Red-eared Slider (illustrated) has a red oval spot behind the eye. In older individuals the colors become blackish and the markings diminish. Pond Sliders are active during the day, when they are fond of basking in groups on logs and rocks near water, sometimes stacked one atop the other, and "sliding" into water for safety if alarmed. Young turtles feed on a variety of small animals, insects, and aquatic invertebrates; adults favor plants. This is the turtle most popular in the pet trade and is now distributed in many areas outside its natural range.

Western Pond Turtle, *Actinemys marmorata*
Family Emydidae (Pond and Box Turtles)
Size: Up to 8" long (carapace)
Range: Along the Pacific coast and inland; Washington to Mexico
Habitat: Ponds, lakes, and streams with muddy bottoms and plentiful aquatic vegetation

The Western Pond Turtle is a mostly aquatic pond turtle with a low, smooth, unkeeled carapace; an unhinged plastron; well-clawed feet; and a blunt head. The carapace is generally dark brown or olive, with thin, radiating yellowish marks or a marbled pattern; or it may lack the patterning and be plainly colored. The plastron is pale yellow; the legs and head are speckled in dark brown, black, and yellow. Males have a contrasting light throat, while the throat of females is dark. They aggressively defend prime basking sites but will leap to safely in the water at the slightest notice of an intruder. They are opportunistic feeders, eating most any available food, including aquatic plants, algae, insects, larvae, crayfish, and carrion.

Eastern Box Turtle, *Terrapene carolina*
Family Emydidae (Pond and Box Turtles)
Size: Up to 6" long (carapace)
Range: Eastern United States, except the far northern latitudes
Habitat: Wet woodlands, fields, meadows, rural gardens

The Eastern Box Turtle has a terrestrial lifestyle, venturing into bogs or wetlands but not open water. It has a tall, domed carapace; a chunky, angular head; and short limbs. It may have three or four toes on the hind feet. It is called a box turtle because the plastron has a lateral "hinge" that allows it to fold up tightly against the carapace, providing complete protection to the turtle's soft parts. The coloration is variable, having contrasting yellow, brown, and black markings in patterns that radiate from a corner of each scute and similar-colored spotting on the head and legs. Eastern Box Turtles feed on slugs, earthworms, plants, fruit, and even poisonous mushrooms, which can make their flesh deadly to eat.

AMPHIBIANS

Northern Cricket Frog, *Acris crepitans*
Family Hylidae (Tree Frogs)
Size: Up to 1½"
Range: Central and eastern United States
Habitat: Warm, shallow streams and ponds

The Northern Cricket frog is a small, ground-dwelling member of the tree frog family. It has bumpy, rough skin and partially webbed rear feet. Its color varies considerably, being some combination of mottled and patchy browns, greens, blacks, and reds, with a paler belly. There is often a distinct triangular mark between its eyes and a whitish stripe below the eyes that extends to the front legs. Though not a climber, the cricket frog is an excellent jumper (it can leap up to 3 feet) and swimmer. Active during the day in water and on the ground, it sometimes basks along shores in groups. The Northern Cricket Frog feeds on small insects and aquatic invertebrates. Its voice is a steely, clicking sound, presumably resembling that of a cricket.

Spring Peeper, *Pseudacris crucifer*
Family Hylidae (Tree Frogs)
Size: Up to 1½" long
Range: Throughout eastern North America; Canada to the Gulf of Mexico
Habitat: Woodlands and grassy areas near ponds or swamps
The Spring Peeper is a small, common tree frog of eastern North America, capable of climbing but mostly found on the ground or in low vegetation. It has some webbing on its feet and enlarged disks on its toes to aid in gripping. Its color can be reddish brown, dark brown, grayish, or olive, with faint dark marks on its upper side and legs and a distinct dark X pattern across the back. Depending on the region, the belly can be plain or spotted. Spring Peepers are active at night, with males perched near the water calling in spring with their familiar high-pitched peeping, jingling chorus. They hunt for a variety of insects and spiders.

American Bullfrog, *Lithobates catesbeiana*
Family Ranidae (True Frogs)
Size: Up to 6"
Range: Throughout central and eastern United States; also along the West Coast and in the Southwest
Habitat: Ponds and lakes with dense vegetation
North America's largest frog, the American Bullfrog is squat and heavy bodied, with massive rear legs that allow quick, strong leaps and strong swimming. Its smooth skin is green to brownish green, with brown or gray mottling or spotting and a pale belly. Its large external eardrums are located just behind the eyes. Bullfrogs are mostly nocturnal and are always found in or near a body of water. Their large mouths enable them to feed on a wide variety of prey, including insects, aquatic invertebrates, and even small mammals and birds.

Southern Leopard Frog, *Lithobates sphenocephalus*
Family Ranidae (True Frogs)
Size: Up to 4" long
Range: South-central United States and East Coast to New York
Habitat: Freshwater or brackish marshes, streams, ponds, moist fields

The Southern Leopard Frog is a squat, boney frog with narrow hindquarters and long, powerful rear legs for leaping. There are two pale narrow ridges of skin along either side of the back and a light stripe above the mouth; the eardrums usually have a light-colored central spot. The overall color of its smooth skin is green to brownish, with large dark spots bordered by a lighter color, giving the frog its common name. Southern Leopard Frogs skulk in the water or vegetation, foraging for insects and invertebrates. Their large mouths allow them to eat fairly large prey, including small birds and other frogs.

Southern Toad, *Anaxyrus terrestris*
Family Bufonidae (Toads)
Size: Up to 3½" long
Range: Throughout coastal plains of southeastern United States
Habitat: Sandy pine-oak woodlands, marshes, rural gardens
The Southern Toad is a medium-size stocky toad with conspicuous protuberances behind the eyes and enlarged oval raised lumps (parotoid glands) behind the eardrums. The skin is dry, covered with warts, and variably brown, gray, or nearly black, with dark spotting and a paler belly (males have a dark throat). Often there is a thin pale dorsal stripe running the length of the back. Southern Toads keep to burrows during the day, emerging at night to feed on insects and other invertebrates. They have an alarming high-pitched, trilled voice.

American Toad, *Bufo americanus*
Family Bufonidae (Toads)
Size: Up to 4" long
Range: Eastern United States except the far South
Habitat: Most moist habitats; woodlands, grassy areas, gardens near a water source

The American Toad is a common toad found throughout residential gardens in the eastern United States. The body is plump and squat, with rough, warty skin and two prominent parotoid glands above and behind the eardrums. The cranial crests between the eyes are not in contact with the parotoid glands and lack the knobs that are present in the similar Southern Toad. The color varies, being some combination of brown, reddish, or olive, with both dark and light spots and mottling and sometimes with a lighter stripe down the back. The belly is spotted. American Toads breed in spring, when males call out with a trilled, cricket-like song. They are most active at night, hiding in vegetation, rocks, or burrows during the day, feasting on insects, spiders, and worms.

Tiger Salamander, *Ambystoma tigrinum*
Family Ambystomatidae (Mole Salamanders)
Size: Up to 13"
Range: Throughout most of the United States except the far West and northeastern states
Habitat: Quite varied: forests, grasslands, sage land, wetlands

The Tiger Salamander is the largest land-dwelling salamander in the world, with a wide variation in color and pattern. The body is robust and rounded; it has a broad, blunt head; small eyes; smooth, shiny skin; and a long tail (longer in males). There are six recognized subspecies, each with a markedly different appearance, ranging from black or brown with yellowish crossbars or whitish spots to pale brown with black barring to pea green with black blotches. Tiger Salamanders spend most of their lives in deep burrows made by rodents, emerging during late-winter rains and migrating to pools or streams to breed. They feed on insects, worms, other amphibians, and small rodents.

Long-toed Salamander, *Ambystoma macrodactylum*
Family Ambystomatidae (Mole Salamanders)
Size: Up to 6½" long
Range: Pacific Northwest; an isolated region near Santa Cruz, California
Habitat: Quite varied; coniferous forests, meadows, dry sagebrush near streams or ponds

The Long-toed Salamander is a small, adaptable mole salamander found from sea level to rocky, high-mountain regions. The body has smooth, shiny skin; a thick base to the head; a slightly flattened tail; and noticeably long, thin toes. The color is black on the back, speckled with white on the sides, and grayish below. Depending on the subspecies, there is a green, yellow, or light brown stripe down the middle of the back that is continuous or broken into spots. Usually active year-round but quite secretive, these salamanders live under rocks, leaf litter, and rotting wood and in burrows; they feed on worms, insects, small fish, and other amphibians. They coil up and twitch their tails when provoked and may detach their tail to distract predators. Otherwise fairly abundant, the Santa Cruz population is critically threatened.

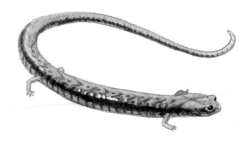

California Slender Salamander, *Batrachoseps attenuatus*
Family Plethodontidae (Lungless Salamanders)
Size: Up to 5½" long
Range: California coastal foothills into southern Oregon; Sierra Nevada
Habitat: Moist woodlands and fields, especially near redwoods

The California Slender Salamander is a small, very thin salamander with a long, rounded tail; small head and eyes; and tiny, thin limbs. As with the other lungless salamanders, it absorbs oxygen through its moist, slimy skin and has distinct costal grooves along the length of its body. Its color is gray brown to black overall, with a paler wide dorsal stripe that varies from brown, reddish, to yellowish and is often marked with thin, darker, forward-pointing chevrons. The belly is dark with fine white specks; the underside of the tail is creamy white. Especially active during periods of rain, slender salamanders lurk among leaf litter and moist logs or roots to hunt for earthworms, spiders, and other invertebrates. They are often found motionless in a tight coil and then quickly and erratically squirm away, even detaching their tail to distract predators.

Eastern Newt, *Notophthalmus viridescens*
Family Salamandridae (Newts)
Size: Up to 3½" long
Range: Throughout eastern United States
Habitat: Wetlands, ponds, nearby meadows or woodlands

Newts are elongate, short-legged, long-tailed, semiaquatic relatives of the salamanders, with dry, rough-textured skin, except in their aquatic phases. They are born in the water, mature on land, and then return to the water as adults. The Eastern Newt comprises several subspecies and has a coloration that varies from orange in the immature stage to greenish brown to blackish in the adult, with a dark orange belly and numerous tiny black spots overall. Newts are adept swimmers, propelled by undulating their bodies and their long flattened tails. They forage day or night in the water or on the ground for insects, larvae, fish or frog eggs, and worms. They may burrow or remain active in the water during winter.

California Newt, *Taricha torosa*
Family Salamandridae (Newts)
Size: Up to 7½" long
Range: California coast and coastal foothills; Sierra Nevada
Habitat: Woodlands of oak, redwood, and pine near streams or ponds

The California Newt is typical of the newts, with its generally dry, rough skin and lack of distinct costal grooves. It has a stocky body and is colored light brown to reddish brown above and yellow orange below, with little contrast in between. The lower eyelids and eyes are pale. During breeding season males develop smooth skin; a flattened tail; dark, rough patches on the inner thigh; and an enlarged vent (anal area). California Newts lurk in leaf litter and burrows made by other animals, roaming farther during rainy weather, and come to a water source to breed. When alarmed, they present a defensive posture, raising their front end and tail to reveal the brightly colored belly and throat. They feed on earthworms, insects, and amphibian eggs.

FISH

Bluegill, *Lepomis macrochirus*
Family Centrarchidae (Sunfish)
Size: Up to 10"
Range: Throughout the United States
Habitat: Shallow lakes and rivers with aquatic plants

Also known as the Bream, the Bluegill is a popular freshwater sport fish. It has an oval, highly compressed body with a small mouth; a dorsal fin that is elongate to the rear; and a slightly forked tail fin. Its color is grayish green above, with indistinct, darker broad vertical bars along the sides, and a dark blue-black patch on the operculum. The underparts are silvery to yellow, becoming red-orange on the chest of the spawning male. Bluegills feed on insects, insect larvae, crustaceans, and small fish. The male is illustrated.

INSECTS

Blue-eyed Darner, *Aeshna multicolor*
Order: Odonata (Dragonflies and Damselflies)
Size: Up to 2½"
Range: Western United States
Habitat: Ponds, streams, wetlands

The darners are among the largest and swiftest dragonflies. Their huge compound eyes encompass most of their head and are joined at the top. The abdomen is long and thin, and the four broad wings are transparent and held outspread while at rest. The body is blackish (in males) or brownish (in females), with blue patterning on the abdomen, blue stripes on the thorax, and iridescent bluish-green eyes. The nymphs are also quite large (2" or more) and live in water, feeding on small invertebrates or small fish and tadpoles. Adult Blue-eyed Darners spend most of the day whizzing through the air catching insects in flight. The adult is illustrated.

Field Crickets (many species)

Order: Orthoptera (Crickets, Grasshoppers, Katydids, and Mantids)
Size: Up to 1"
Range: Throughout North America
Habitat: A wide variety of moist habitats; in brush and leaf litter, under rocks and logs

The name "Field Cricket" has been applied to several different species of crickets, all of which are quite similar in appearance. They have a somewhat flattened body, tough wings, long and thin antennae, large rear legs, and a pair of forked appendages (cerci) that protrude from the end of the abdomen. In females there is also a long tubular structure (the ovipositor) through which eggs are laid. Field Crickets are almost always black, unlike the paler color of House Crickets. They scurry through underbrush and moist places during the night, feeding on a wide variety of plant or invertebrate prey, including eggs of other insects. During mid-summer the males begin their familiar, high-pitched trilling calls caused by rubbing a specialized part of their wing. This attracts females, who will deposit eggs in the soil or in plant tissue.

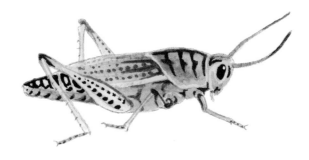

Eastern Lubber Grasshopper, *Romalea microptera*
Order: Orthoptera (Crickets, Grasshoppers, Katydids, and Mantids)
Size: Up to 2½"
Range: Southeastern United States
Habitat: Fields, rural gardens, disturbed areas

The Eastern Lubber Grasshopper is one of many members of the group known as "short-horned grasshoppers" due to their relatively short, stubby antennae. Its body has a long abdomen and shield-like upper thorax (pronotum), the eyes are large, and the mouth has strong, chewing mouthparts. Although equipped with large hind legs like other grasshoppers and crickets, it is not a particularly good jumper, but rather it lumbers sluggishly along the ground and vegetation. Also, because its wings are so short, it is incapable of flight. The color may be yellow to reddish brown with intricate black markings, or nearly solid black with a yellow edging on the back of the pronotum and on the abdomen. These large plant eaters can occur in huge numbers and are often considered pests to farmers and gardeners. A light-phase adult is illustrated.

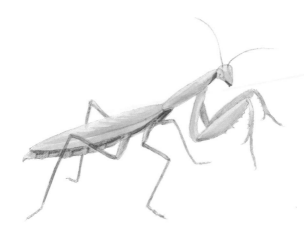

Praying Mantis, *Mantis religiosa*
Order: Orthoptera (Crickets, Grasshoppers, Katydids, and Mantids)
Size: Up to 2½"
Range: Eastern and northwestern United States
Habitat: Gardens, fields

Also known as the European Mantid, the Praying Mantis was introduced to North America from Europe in the late 1800s and is now common and welcome in gardens and flowerbeds across the United States. This is a long, slender insect with thin legs, an extended thorax region, and a relatively small, triangular head with big eyes and lacy antennae. Most obvious are the large spined forelegs with a longer than usual inner segment. The color can range from green to brownish, with a dark ringed spot on the inner part of the foreleg base. Praying Mantises hunt by waiting motionless with the front legs raised in a "praying" position, then quickly grasping prey when it is in range. All manner of insects, their larvae, and spiders are eaten, including other mantids. Females create a papery egg case on twigs, which overwinters and produces a hundred or more tiny young in the spring.

Jerusalem Cricket, *Stenopelmatus fuscus*

Order: Orthoptera (Crickets, Grasshoppers, Katydids, and Mantids)
Size: Up to 2"
Range: Western United States
Habitat: Dark, moist places in soil, leaf litter, under rocks

Although fearsome in appearance, the Jerusalem Cricket is not poisonous or dangerous, although it has been known to deliver a mild bite if threatened. Because it looks almost like a fat, oversize ant, it also goes by a number of common names including "old bald-headed man," "child of the earth," "skull insect," and "potato bug." Its abdomen is plump and clearly segmented; its head is large, round, and smooth with beady black eyes; and its limbs are compact and have spines to aid in digging. It has no wings. The Jerusalem Cricket's color is glossy amber brown with dark brown bands over the abdomen. These crickets are active mostly at night, feeding on decaying organic matter on the ground, burrowing into the soil for plant tubers, or wandering into homes. It can make a hissing sound by rubbing its back legs against the body, or a thumping sound by tapping its abdomen against the ground.

American Cockroach, *Periplaneta americana*
Order: Blattodea (Cockroaches)
Size: Up to 2"
Range: Worldwide
Habitat: Woodlands of subtropical habitats, urban areas, buildings, sewers

Although an important insect in the subtropical ecosystems where it lives wild, the American Cockroach is best known as a creepy pest that inhabits nooks and crevices of homes and other buildings throughout North America. The body is oval shaped and flattened, with overlapping wings that cover the entire back (wings are larger in males than in females). The head is small and usually obscured by the large pronotum (front of the thorax), and the antennae are thin and longer than the body. Two appendages at the rear (cerci) are well developed. Its color is reddish brown overall, with a paler band across the pronotum. Cockroaches are active mostly during the night, crawling and sometimes flying in search of almost any food source. In the wild they seek out hidden places under rocks and logs; in buildings their flattened shape allows them to squeeze into the thinnest spaces between wood panels and cement walls.

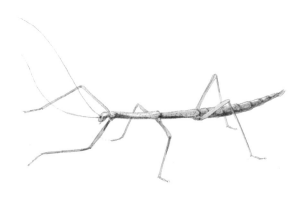

Northern Walkingstick, *Diapheromera femorata*
Order: Phasmatodea (Walkingsticks)
Size: Up to 3½"
Range: Central and eastern United States
Habitat: Deciduous woodlands, gardens, parks

Also known as the Common American Walkingstick, these curious insects are uncanny in their resemblance to twigs, sticks, and vines as they stand motionless or even sway gently to mimic a breeze. This camouflage allows them to remain virtually undetected to predators, especially when the limbs are held close to the body. As a further defense, they can detach a limb, which regenerates in a subsequent molt. The body is elongate and tubular, like a twig, with a small squarish head and very thin long legs. It has no wings. The color is brown (in males), brown with a bit of green (in females), or overall green (in juveniles). Walkingsticks feed on the leaves of deciduous trees and shrubs, mostly at night for safety, slowly munching an entire leaf before moving on to the next. Their bizarre appearance and gentle nature have made them popular as pets. The male is illustrated.

European Earwig, *Forficula auricularia*
Order: Dermaptera (Earwigs)
Size: Up to ⅝"
Range: Northern United States
Habitat: Variable habitats with moist, dark hiding places; gardens, fields

Many people are squeamish around earwigs, but their fears are unfounded, as these insects are perfectly harmless to humans. They do not crawl into people's ears, and the pincers at the rear end are used as self-defense against small predators but are much too weak to harm humans. The European Earwig was introduced from Europe and now inhabits most temperate climates of the United States. The body is elongate, dark reddish brown above and yellowish below and on the legs and antennae. The hind pincers are robust and curved in males but relatively straight and thin in females. Short wings are present, but these earwigs rarely fly. They are active mostly at night, when they search for bits of plants or small insects in leaf litter, the soil, or up the stems of plants. Occasionally they will find their way into homes through small cracks and feed on foods therein. The male is illustrated.

Green Stink Bug, *Acrosternum hilare*
Order: Hemiptera (True Bugs)
Size: Up to ¾"
Range: Throughout North America
Habitat: Woodlands, gardens, meadows

The Green Stink Bug is a member of the order of "true bugs" (Hemiptera), all of which have forewings that fold neatly over the back and are leathery at the basal half and membranous at the outer half. It also has a triangular patch on the top of its thorax between the wings. Its body is broad and flattened, like a little shield, with small legs and a small head. It is overall bright green, often edged with yellow or red along the body's perimeter, and has black bands on the antennae. It uses well-developed sucking mouthparts to extract the juices of all kinds of plant material, including commercial crops and home gardens, where it can be a major pest. Its common name is due to the fact that adults and larvae can emit a foul-smelling fluid in defense.

Harlequin Bug, *Murgantia histrionica*
Order: Hemiptera (True Bugs)
Size: Up to ⅜"
Range: Lower latitudes throughout the United States
Habitat: Fields, gardens, meadows

The Harlequin Bug is a member of the group known as "stink bugs" because of the foul-smelling odor they emit. Also known as "cabbage bugs" or "fire bugs," they are broad, short, and shaped like a small shield. Its upper side is attractively patterned in yellow orange and deep black, and its folded wings produce the traditional X shape across the abdomen (common to the Hemiptera, or true bugs). Tiny eggs are laid in rows on the underside of leaves and look like black-and-white–ringed barrels. Growing nymphs and adults suck the sap of many garden and crop plants such as cabbage, mustard, tomatoes, and beets, often causing serious damage.

Water Boatmen, *Corixa* spp.
Order: Hemiptera (True Bugs)
Size: Up to ½"
Range: Throughout North America
Habitat: Ponds, streams

Water Boatmen are aquatic members of the true bug group that can be found in almost any body of stagnant fresh or brackish water, including swimming pools, birdbaths, and puddles. Its body is elongate and oval, with a flattened, streamlined shape, and the small antennae fold neatly into grooves on the head. Its front legs are reduced, while its rear legs are enlarged, with feathery outer sections that serve as paddles for forward propulsion. Its color is pale to dark gray brown, with many thin, black transverse striations. Water Boatmen dart through the water near the bottom or cling to aquatic plants. They feed on algae or bits of detritus, using their small front legs as a scoop. They are capable of making high-pitched chirps by rubbing their forelegs against their head. Unlike another group of aquatic bugs, the Backswimmers, Water Boatmen do not bite people.

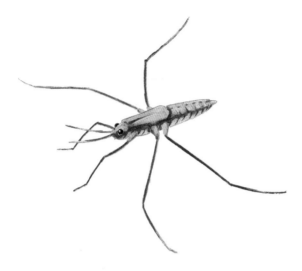

Common Water Strider, *Aquarius remigis*

Order: Hemiptera (True Bugs)
Size: Up to ½"
Range: Throughout North America
Habitat: Ponds, streams, wetlands

Water striders, as a group, are fascinating aquatic bugs that are almost always in motion, darting across the surface of shallow waters. Sometimes called "skaters" or "Jesus bugs," they can literally walk on water by using excellent weight distribution of their legs, which are lined with tiny water-repelling hairs, and the physics of surface tension. The Common Water Strider is relatively small with a narrow blackish body, a pair of short grasping legs, and very long, thin middle and hind legs. They eat a variety of planktonic food and are capable of subduing larger insects as well, from which they suck the juices with specialized mouthparts.

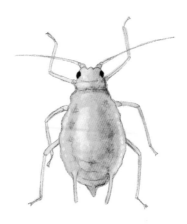

Green Peach Aphid, *Myzus persicae*
Order: Homoptera (Aphids, Cicadas, and Allies)
Size: Up to ⅛"
Range: Throughout North America
Habitat: Orchards, gardens near trees in the peach family, including plum, cherry, and apricot

Aphids comprise a group of thousands of species throughout the world. They are typically quite small with soft bodies, thin legs, long antennae, a taillike appendage, and tubular growths called cornicles on either side of the back. The Green Peach Aphid is yellowish green, but winged forms are also black on the head and thorax. They feed on sap in the plant tissue of a wide variety of garden plants and trees by inserting a specialized sucking mouthpart called a stylet into the plant and then discharging a sticky, sugary fluid known as honeydew. Because they are able to reproduce asexually, populations can grow very fast and become major pests. However, they are an important food source for many other insects, especially Ladybird Beetles and their larvae. Some aphid colonies are tended by ants, who protect them in exchange for a constant supply of honeydew.

Grand Western Cicada, *Tibicen dorsata*

Order: Homoptera (Aphids, Cicadas, and Allies)
Size: Up to 1½"
Range: Southwestern and central United States
Habitat: Woodlands, fields, rural gardens

Cicadas are large, chunky insects with bulbous eyes, tiny legs, and two pairs of membranous, thick-veined wings that are much longer than their body. The Grand Western Cicada, also known as the "bush cicada" or "grassland cicada," is handsomely marked in patterns of black, brown, and white, with clear wings that have brownish veins. The wings are held angled, tentlike, when at rest. Male cicadas are capable of producing a surprisingly loud buzz or whining sound with specialized organs under their abdomens, and they most commonly do so late in the day during the late summer months. The nymphs, after hatching, burrow into the ground and feed on plant roots and can live for several years in this stage. Eventually they emerge and molt on a nearby tree trunk to become mature adults, who live only a few weeks. The empty shells of the final molt are often seen clinging to bark.

Convergent Ladybird Beetle, *Hippodamia convergens*
Order: Coleoptera (Beetles)
Size: Up to ⅜"
Range: Eastern United States
Habitat: Gardens, fields, woodlands

The ladybird beetles, commonly called "ladybugs" (although they are not true bugs), comprise a large group of familiar and welcome beetles that are voracious predators on many destructive insects such as aphids and scale insects. Most are small, nearly round and domed above; have tiny legs and antennae; and are colored orange to reddish with variable black spots. The Convergent Ladybird Beetle is shiny red with thirteen black spots on its back and a black pronotum (top of the thorax) with a white border and two converging white stripes. The larva is spindly, spiny, and black with orange spots, and it forms a pupa that is orangey with black spots. Adults may overwinter in large numbers under clumps of leaves, becoming active again in the spring. Ladybird beetles are sometimes bought and released as a biological pest-control device in gardens and crops.

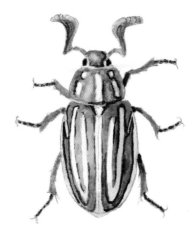

Ten-lined June Beetle, *Polyphylla decimlineata*
Order: Coleoptera (Beetles)
Size: Up to 1½"
Range: Western United States
Habitat: Woodlands, fields, gardens

The Ten-lined June Beetle is a member of a large group known as the "scarab beetles," all relatively large and robust with big heads, powerful front legs for digging, and curious, platelike antennae that can be fanned out or folded into a compact ball. It is mottled golden brown and black above, with distinct white lines along the shell-like forewings on the back and thorax. The underside is lined with fuzzy tan or reddish hairs. The larva is pale, grub-like, and curved into a C shape and lives underground. It can be a serious pest where it feeds on the roots of plants or young trees. Adults are most active at night in warm weather, flying low over fields, and are attracted to lights.

Common Black Ground Beetle, *Pterostichus melanarius*
Order: Coleoptera (Beetles)
Size: Up to ⅝"
Range: Throughout North America
Habitat: Gardens, woodlands, fields

Ground beetles are members of the family Carabidae (known as the "carab beetles") and consist of thousands of species. Most are shiny black or of iridescent colors with prominent thoraxes, long and thin legs, and narrow heads. Although capable of flight, they typically speed away on foot rather than fly when threatened. The Common Black Ground Beetle was introduced from Europe and is now common in much of North America. Its color is glossy black overall, and the forewings, folded neatly over the back, are grooved. They spend the day hiding under stones and logs and become active at night, pursuing small insects and slugs on the ground or on plants. They are generally considered beneficial in gardens and crops, although they can emit a foul-smelling substance if handled.

Pyralis Firefly, *Photinus pyralis*
Order: Coleoptera (Beetles)
Size: Up to ½"
Range: Eastern and central United States
Habitat: Meadows, swamps

Fireflies, also known as "lightning bugs," are actually a kind of small beetle. They are most active on spring and summer nights, when they delight viewers with blinking flashes of light, the pattern of which varies with different species. A special chemical process in the last sections of the abdomen creates this yellow-green glow, and it is found in the larvae as well. The Pyralis Firefly's body is soft and elongate, with small legs and a large pronotum (top of the thorax) that conceals the head when seen from above. The back is black with thin orange stripes down the center and sides. The pronotum is yellow around the edges with a red interior, and it has a black mark in the center. Adults rarely feed, but larvae prey on small insects, slugs, and worms, which they find under logs and in moist leaf litter.

Pipevine Swallowtail, *Battus philenor*
Order: Lepidoptera (Butterflies and Moths)
Size: Wingspan 3–5"
Range: Southern latitudes across the contiguous United States and into Mexico
Habitat: Woodland edges, streamsides, open fields
The Pipevine Swallowtail is a dark, medium-size, active swallow-tail with shallowly scalloped hind wings and moderate tail pro-jections. It is poisonous to predators and thus often mimicked by other butterfly species. The upper side of the forewing is flat black and iridescent, while the upper surface of the hind wing is metal-lic blue (more developed in males) with pale crescent-shaped spots along its base. The underside hind wing has large, orange submarginal spots and retains the blue sheen of its upper surface. The body is black with small yellow spots along the sides, and the antennae are thin with clubbed tips. The caterpillar is dark, reddish brown, smooth, and lined with fleshy appendages and orange spots. It eats the leaves of pipevines and related plants. The adult feeds on flower nectar and nutrients from mud puddles.

Eastern Tiger Swallowtail, *Papilio glaucus*

Order: Lepidoptera (Butterflies and Moths)
Size: Wingspan 3–5½"
Range: Throughout eastern United States
Habitat: Gardens, parks, riversides, forest clearings

Among the largest of North American butterflies, the Eastern Tiger Swallowtail is common throughout its range, is diurnal, and—typical of this family—has distinct projections, or "tails," on the hind wings. When the butterfly is alighted and/or feeding, the wings may be seen to tremble. Both sexes are bright yellow above and show ragged black stripes, like those of a tiger, along the anterior forewings and black marginal patterning on both forewings and hind wings. The first submarginal spot on the hind wing is orange. The underside is patterned similarly but is much paler yellow. Females show bright blue posterior markings, and in some southern individuals may be nearly black overall (and look similar to the Spicebush Swallowtail). Like the wings, the body has black and yellow stripes. The caterpillar is brown to greenish, smooth, and plump. The caterpillar eats the leaves of trees, including those from the rose, magnolia, laurel, and willow families. Adults feed on flower nectar and the salts and moisture from puddles. The adult female is illustrated.

Orange Sulfur, *Colias eurytheme*
Order: Lepidoptera (Butterflies and Moths)
Size: Wingspan 1½–2½"
Range: Throughout the contiguous United States
Habitat: Meadows, fields, farmlands, roadsides

Also known as the Alfalfa Butterfly, this common butterfly is often found in dense, low-flying groups over alfalfa fields, where it is often considered a pest. The upper-side wings are yellow and extensively washed with bright orange. A wide dark band occurs along the outer margins of both the forewings and hind wings, a reddish discal spot appears on the hind wing, and a distinct black discal spot sits on the forewing. The dark margin in females is broken by irregular orange markings. The butterfly's underside is yellow with a red-bordered white discal spot on the hind wing, accompanied by a smaller spot just above it. Its body is pale yellow below and darker above, and the club-tipped antennae are reddish. The caterpillar is thin, smooth, and green, with a pale longitudinal stripe down each side. This species is similar to the Clouded, or Common, Sulfur, which has a lemon-yellow rather than orange cast and lacks the hind wing spot. The caterpillar eats alfalfa and clover. Adults feed on flower nectar. The illustration shows the adult male.

Cabbage Butterfly, *Pieris rapae*
Order: Lepidoptera (Butterflies and Moths)
Size: Wingspan 1⅜–1¾"
Range: Throughout the contiguous United States
Habitat: Open fields, farmlands, roadsides

Also known as the Cabbage White or Small White, the Cabbage Butterfly is a hardy, nonnative species introduced to North America in the late 1800s and now found across the continent. The upper-side wings are plain, creamy white with gray to black apical patches and show a distinct dark spot on the center of the forewings and upper margins of the hind wings. Females have an additional spot on the forewing, below the first. The underside is pale yellow to yellow green. Early broods of this species tend to be paler with fewer dark markings than late broods. Its body is dark above, paler below, with long hairs, especially on the thorax. The antennae are thin and club tipped. The caterpillar is pale green with thin, longitudinal yellow stripes and a delicate, bumpy-hairy surface. The caterpillar eats cabbage and other plants of the mustard (Brassicaceae) family, including *Nasturtium* sp. Also known as a "cabbage worm," it is considered a major pest to crops. Adults feed on flower nectar. The illustration shows the adult female.

American Copper, *Lycaena phlaeas*
Order: Lepidoptera (Butterflies and Moths)
Size: Wingspan 1–1¼"
Range: Throughout the contiguous United States, but most commonly in northern and eastern regions
Habitat: Meadows, roadsides, fields

The American Copper is a small, beautiful common butterfly with a fairly aggressive disposition. The wing patterning is variable, but generally the upper-side forewing is coppery orange with a dark marginal band and several black spots. The hind wing is mostly blackish or dark brown with an orange basal band. A thin, pale margin is present on both sets of wings. The underside wings are similar but much paler overall. The sexes are similar, although some females may show bluish markings above the orange band on the hind wing. Its body is dark brown above, pale grayish below, with dark, club-tipped antennae dotted with white. The caterpillar is like a slug, variously colored pale greenish to reddish and covered with fine hairs. The caterpillar feeds on various sorrels and docks. Adults feed on flower nectar. The adult female is illustrated.

Monarch, *Danaus plexippus*
Order: Lepidoptera (Butterflies and Moths)
Size: Wingspan 3–4½"
Range: Throughout the contiguous United States to north-central Mexico
Habitat: Sunny, open fields as well as meadows and gardens; during migration can be found in almost any environment

The Monarch is a large, sturdy, long-lived butterfly best known for one of the most incredible migratory journeys of the animal kingdom—its yearly flight to Mexico, in which millions of this species gather in discrete, isolated locations. The upper sides of the wings are deep orange with wide, black stripes along the veins and black margins infused with a double row of white spots. Males have narrower black vein markings than females, as well as a small dark "sex spot" near the base of each hind wing. The underside is marked as above, but the orange is paler. The body is black with white spots on the head and thorax, with thin, club-tipped antennae. The caterpillar is fat, smooth, and ringed with black, white, and yellow bands and has black tentacles behind its head. The caterpillar eats leaves and flowers of milkweed. Adults feed on flower nectar. Both store toxins from milkweed that make them distasteful to predators. The adult male is shown.

Painted Lady, *Vanessa cardui*
Order: Lepidoptera (Butterflies and Moths)
Size: Wingspan 2–2½"
Range: Throughout the contiguous United States
Habitat: Open habitats, gardens, fields, alpine meadows

The Painted Lady is a medium-size, wide-ranging common butterfly that can be found around the world, so it is sometimes called the Cosmopolitan. It has strong but erratic flight and is capable of long migrations. The upper-side wings are pale orange-brown with extensive black markings. A black apical region on the forewing contains several white spots, and small blue spots may be visible at the inner base of the hind wing. The underside forewing is patterned as above, but the hind wing is mottled in earth tones with a row of submarginal eyespots. The body is speckled light and dark brown above, is whitish below, and has thin, club-tipped antennae ending in pale dots. The caterpillar is blackish with pale yellow stripes and is covered in fine hairs and bristles. It eats a wide variety of plants, including thistles, nettles, burdock, hollyhock, and mallow, enabling it to thrive in most areas. Adults feed on flower nectar.

Buckeye, *Junonia coenia*
Order: Lepidoptera (Butterflies and Moths)
Size: Wingspan 1¾–2½"
Range: Throughout the contiguous United States, most commonly in southern latitudes
Habitat: Open fields, meadows, coastal shores
The Buckeye is a medium-size common butterfly with pro-nounced eyespots, which are thought to confuse and deter pred-ators. It tends to remain on or near the ground or low parts of vegetation. The upper-side wings are variable shades of brown, with each wing showing one large and one small multicolored spot. There is also a creamy bar near the apex of the forewing, two orange marks in the discal cell, and scalloped patterning along the entire wing edge. The underside is paler, sometimes achiev-ing a rose cast, with eyespots still visible. The body is tan to dark brown, with pale, club-tipped antennae. The caterpillar is mottled black, white, and brown, with dark stripes above, and is covered in black branched spines. The caterpillar eats the leaves, buds, and fruit of plantains, gerardias, and snapdragons. Adults feed on flower nectar and moisture from mud and sand.

Mourning Cloak, *Nymphalis antiopa*
Order: Lepidoptera (Butterflies and Moths)
Size: Wingspan 2¼–3½"
Range: Throughout temperate North America
Habitat: Deciduous woodlands, parks, rural gardens

The Mourning Cloak is a common butterfly with the angular, jagged wing margins typical of the tortoiseshells. The adult overwinters in tree cavities, emerging the following spring to breed. The upper-side wings are deep burgundy brown with wide, pale yellow margins. Inside the margin are light blue spots surrounded by black. The underside is dark gray with the same yellowish margin, though on this side it is speckled with black. The body is stout and dark brown to blackish both above and below, with thin, club-tipped antennae. The caterpillar is black, covered with spines, and has small white dots and a row of reddish spots along the back. It eats the leaves of a variety of broadleaf trees, including willow, poplar, elm, birch, and hackberry. Adults feed on rotting fruit, tree sap, flower nectar (rarely), and moisture and salts from soil.

Polyphemus Moth, *Antheraea polyphemus*
Order: Lepidoptera (Butterflies and Moths)
Size: Wingspan 3½–5¾"
Range: Throughout the contiguous United States
Habitat: Deciduous woodlands, gardens

The Polyphemus Moth is a very large, common silkmoth with a stout, heavily furred body. It is named for the mythical Cyclops Polyphemus, who had a single eye. The upper-side wings are light to dark brown overall. The forewing has a small black-bordered and white discal eyespot, small black apical patches, a dark sub-marginal line, and a reddish basal stripe. The hind wing has very large black eyespots encircling yellow and a broad, dark submarginal stripe. The underside is paler overall with only a suggestion of eyespots. The body is brownish overall, above and below, with feathered antennae that are more pronounced in the male. The caterpillar is bright green with a brown head, banded with thin yellow stripes and dotted with orange tubercles bearing thin dark spines. The caterpillar eats leaves from a variety of broadleaf trees, including oak, willow, apple, hawthorn, and birch. Adults do not feed. The illustration shows the adult male.

Regal Moth, *Citheronia regalis*
Order: Lepidoptera (Butterflies and Moths)
Size: Wingspan 3½–6"
Range: Throughout eastern United States, especially southeast
Habitat: Deciduous woodlands, gardens, parks

The Regal Moth, also known as the Royal Walnut Moth, is a massive, large-bodied moth. The upper-side wings have a gray-to-brown background color with scattered pale yellow spots on the inner portion; the margins are unmarked. The hind wing is paler and more orange, while the forewing has unusual red-orange veins. Females are larger than males. The body is well furred and thick, striped reddish and pale yellow on the thorax, and banded on the abdomen. The legs are red orange, and the antennae are relatively small and feathery. The caterpillar, known as the "hickory horned devil," is very large and imposing, green, and marked with black spots and lines and has several long, arching, red-orange horns on the head and thorax. The caterpillar eats leaves from a variety of trees from the walnut family (Juglandaceae), including hickory, walnut, sweet gum, and pecan. Adults do not feed.

Sheep Moth, *Hemileuca eglanterina*
Order: Lepidoptera (Butterflies and Moths)
Size: Wingspan 2–3"
Range: West of the Continental Divide in the contiguous United States, most especially California and northwestern states
Habitat: A variety of habitats including coastal areas, mountains, woodlands, pastures, and scrubland

The Sheep Moth, also known as the Elegant Sheep Moth, is a silk moth of the West that can be found flying during the day. The wing pattern and coloration are extremely variable. Generally this moth is rosy to pink on the forewing and yellow orange on the hind wing, with both wings showing large, central black spots, marginal streaks, and transverse bands. In some regions, however, the dark markings are more extensive, reduced, or entirely absent. The underside wings are patterned as above. The body is long for a silk moth, with a thin abdomen. It is yellow to pinkish with a black-banded abdomen and feathered antennae (broader in the male). The caterpillar is blackish, often with dorsal red spots and white lines along the sides, and has rows of highly branched orange and black spines. The caterpillar eats plants from the rose family (Rosaceae), Ceanothus, willow, and aspen. Adults do not feed. The illustration shows the male.

White-lined Sphinx, *Hyles lineata*

Order: Lepidoptera (Butterflies and Moths)
Size: Wingspan 2½–3½"
Range: Widespread throughout the contiguous United States
Habitat: A variety of habitats including fields, gardens, and dry scrub

The White-lined Sphinx, worldwide in distribution, is sometimes referred to as the Striped Morning Sphinx because it flies during the day as well as night. It is large bodied with a tapered abdomen and pointed, narrow wings. The upper side of the forewing is tan and dark brown with a broad pale stripe from the wing base to the tip, crossed by broad white veins. The hind wing is mostly pink with black at the base and just inside the outer margin. The underside wings are paler overall. The head and upper thorax of the body are brownish with white stripes, while the abdomen has black-and-white spotting along the top and sides. The antennae are long, with compact feathering. The caterpillar is plump, smooth, and blackish; shows variable amounts of yellow or green stripes and spots; and has a prominent, yellow-orange tail horn. The caterpillar eats a variety of plants, including apple, elm, evening primrose, and tomato. Adults feed on flower nectar, using their very long proboscises to probe deep into flowers.

Hummingbird Clearwing, *Hemaris thysbe*
Order: Lepidoptera (Butterflies and Moths)
Size: Wingspan 1½–2½"
Range: From Alaska to Florida, most commonly in eastern and rarely in southwestern United States
Habitat: Gardens, meadows, roadsides

The Hummingbird Clearwing is a common, medium-size hawk moth that is active during the day and resembles a small hummingbird with its rapid, hovering flight and compact body shape. The forewings are narrow and pointed, are reddish brown with olive green at the base, and have large, clear, scaleless patches along their central sections. The hind wings are much smaller and rounded, with similar clear patches. The body is robust, with olive green above on the thorax and head, whitish below, with dark reddish brown to blackish on the abdomen that terminates in a broad tail tuft. The antennae are long, thick, and black. The caterpillar is fat and bright green, with longitudinal pale stripes and a single yellow to bluish tail horn. The caterpillar eats a variety of plants, including hawthorn, honeysuckle, cherry, plum, and snowberry. The adults feed on flower nectar, using a long proboscis to probe deep into flowers.

Eight-spotted Forester, *Alypia octomaculata*
Order: Lepidoptera (Butterflies and Moths)
Size: Wingspan 1–1½"
Range: Throughout the United States, most commonly in eastern states
Habitat: Open woodlands, fields, riparian areas, urban parks

The Eight-spotted Forester is a small, boldly patterned moth with strong flight that is active during the day. The upper-side wings are rich black overall, with two large, pale yellow spots on the forewing and two large, white spots on the hind wing, although there may be variation in the number and size of these markings. The undersides of the wings are patterned just like the upper sides. The body is black overall, with pale yellow sides to the thorax, variably occurring white spotting on top of the abdomen, bright orange tufts on the front two legs, and dark antennae that thicken toward the tip but are not noticeably feathered. The caterpillar is black with broad orange bands and thin, broken white bands and is spiked with thin pale hairs. The caterpillar eats a variety of plants, including grape, Virginia creeper, woodvine, and peppervine. Adults feed on flower nectar.

Garden Tiger Moth, *Arctia caja*

Order: Lepidoptera (Butterflies and Moths)
Size: Wingspan 2–2¾"
Range: Primarily the Pacific Northwest and Rocky Mountains, but also found in north-central and northeastern states
Habitat: A variety of habitats, especially damp areas, meadows, and streamsides

The Garden Tiger Moth is a beautiful, medium-size tiger moth with nocturnal habits and quite variable wing coloration. In general the upper side of the forewing consists of a contrasting mosaic of reddish or dark brown patches over a white background. The hind wing is bright orange with large, black-rimmed blue spots and a pale margin. With the forewings folded down, the butterfly is camouflaged in grasses and brush, but when alarmed it flashes its brilliant hind wings to frighten predators. The body is dark brown above on the head and thorax, with a red collar at the neck, and is orange with broken, dark blue bands on the abdomen. It is mostly brownish orange below, with pale, compact antennae. The caterpillar is of the "woolly bear" type, densely covered in long, pale-tipped black bristles with shorter reddish bristles near the base and at the neck. The caterpillar eats a wide variety of herbaceous and woody plants, including blackberry, clover, plum, plantain, birch, and apple.

Isabella Tiger Moth, *Pyrrharctia isabella*
Order: Lepidoptera (Butterflies and Moths)
Size: Wingspan 1¾–2½"
Range: Throughout the contiguous United States
Habitat: Open deciduous woodlands, grasslands, gardens, parks

The Isabella Tiger Moth is a common, medium-size moth, most often known by its larval form, the woolly bear caterpillar. The adult has relatively long, pointed forewings, which are colored light yellow brown overall and sparsely marked with faint bars near the outer and medial sections. There are also variable numbers of small dark spots on the interior and outer margins. The hind wing of the female is tinged orange to pink, whereas that of the male is pale yellow. The body is orange-brown, with a hairy, tufted upper thorax; dark spots along the upper abdomen; thin, pale antennae; and black legs. The caterpillar is plump and covered with fuzzy fine hairs. It is black with a wide orange-brown central section. The caterpillar eats a wide variety of herbaceous and woody plants, including maples, clover, sunflowers, elm, and grasses.

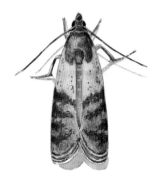

Indian Meal Moth, *Plodia interpunctella*

Order: Lepidoptera (Butterflies and Moths)
Size: Wingspan ½–¾"
Range: Worldwide
Habitat: Indoor places with a food source, especially kitchens, pantries, and warehouses, or outside in warm climates (they do not tolerate cold)

The Indian Meal Moth is a native of South America that has become naturalized across the globe from the transport of foods that contain its eggs and larvae. It is also known as the Pantry Moth and is a considerable pest in homes and anywhere dried foods are stored. The adult is tiny, with narrow forewings that are pale gray brown at the base, dark reddish brown on the outer half, and overlaid with broad, broken, charcoal-gray transverse bands. The hind wing is uniformly off-white, but it is usually hidden by the tightly folded forewings. The surface of both wings may show a metallic sheen. The body is brown above, gray below, with long, thin antennae. The caterpillar, known as a "waxworm," is smooth and shiny, white, creamy, or pale gray, with a brown head. Feeding caterpillars will leave a residue of silk webbing inside the food source. The caterpillar eats various grains (especially cornmeal, from which its common name is derived), cereals, dried foods, and pet food. Adults do not feed.

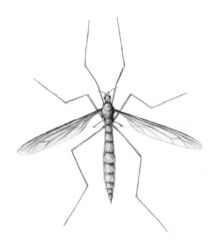

Crane Flies, *Tipula* spp.

Order: Diptera (Flies)
Size: Up to 1"
Range: Throughout North America
Habitat: Varied habitats, usually near water or moist soils; gardens, fields, indoors

Crane flies appear like giant mosquitoes, but are completely harmless. Many species inhabit North America, all of which have extremely long thin legs (easily broken off); a long thin abdomen; a broad thorax; long antennae; and one pair of thin wings. In place of rear wings, there is a pair of small projections that aid in balance. Their color is drab gray or brownish. Females are sometimes wingless and have a thin, egg-laying projection (the ovipositor) at the rear (this is not a stinger, as some might fear). The larvae are like grubs, with tough leathery skin, and feed on decaying plant matter and fungi, although some are pests of garden and crop plants. Adults rarely feed and commonly come indoors, where they lazily cling to curtains or window sidings.

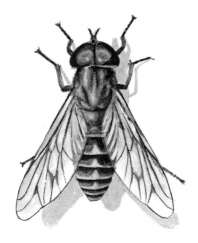

Horse Flies, *Tabanus* spp.
Order: Diptera (Flies)
Size: Up to 1"
Range: Throughout North America
Habitat: Most habitats near a water source; woodlands, marshes

Horse flies are related to the deer flies but are generally much larger. Their feeding habits are similar, however, slicing a small incision into the host and sucking out the blood, and they can be a serious pest to livestock. The body is robust, with broad, black and green eyes and short, amber-colored, hornlike antennae. The thorax and abdomen are grayish to brownish, with weakly patterned paler areas at each abdominal segment. The wings are mostly clear with dark veins. An egg mass is laid on surfaces above water or on a moist substrate, and larvae feed on larval insects or worms in the soil. Adults are active during the day in the late summer months and live for only a matter of days.

Mosquitoes (many species)
Order: Diptera (Flies)
Size: Up to ¼"
Range: Throughout North America
Habitat: Nearly all habitats close to a water source

Well-known to everyone, mosquitoes are a large group of delicate flies with thousands of known species. In general they have small, elongate bodies; long, thin legs; thin wings with small scales; and a long, sharp proboscis. Females have feathery, plume-like antennae, while males have narrower, bristled antennae. Females feed on the blood of vertebrates, including humans, by secreting a saliva (which is responsible for causing itching) and sucking blood through their proboscis. Males feed on nectar and plant juices. Eggs are laid on the surface of any body of stagnant water, and the larvae, called "wrigglers," float on the water and breathe air through a small tube. These morph into another stage, the pupa, which does not feed. Adults are most active during twilight hours or at night. They are major vectors of disease such as malaria and yellow fever. The male of the *Aedes* genus is illustrated.

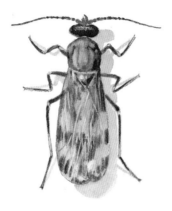

Biting Midges, *Culicoides* spp.
Order: Diptera (Flies)
Size: Up to ⅛"
Range: Throughout North America
Habitat: Wetlands, ponds, streams

Also known as "punkies" or "no-see-ums" because of their tiny size, biting midges gather in swarms and annoy campers and fishers with their cumulative, irritating bits. Unlike true midges, they hold their wings across the back instead of outstretched when at rest. The body resembles a small, compact mosquito, with a bulbous abdomen that swells during feeding and a small head that is positioned lower than the thorax. They are colored grayish to pale green, with light and dark patterned wings. The larvae are pale and wormlike and live in or near water or other moist environments. Adults feed on nectar or vertebrate blood, or they attack other insects.

Little Black Ant, *Monomorium minimum*
Order: Hymenoptera (Ants, Bees, and Wasps)
Size: Up to ⅟₁₆"
Range: Throughout North America
Habitat: Woodlands, rural areas, houses

Little Black Ants are common, tiny ants that are probably best known for finding their way into kitchens or pantries in search of food scraps. They have a complex social structure, with a queen (or queens) that produces eggs and workers that tend to the young and collect food for the colony. Workers are shiny black or dark brown and wingless, with elbowed antennae. The narrow waist, or pedicel, has two segments (although you need a magnifying glass to see this). When a worker ant locates food, it communicates its find to other ants, and soon a trail of workers is formed from the food source to the colony. Colonies are located underground, in rotting woodpiles, or in voids in foundations and patios. The small size of these ants allows them to move through even the narrowest cracks in walls and flooring.

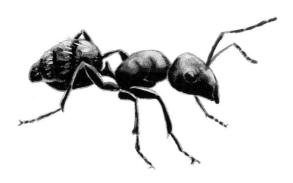

Black Carpenter Ant, *Camponotus pennsylvanicus*
Order: Hymenoptera (Ants, Bees, and Wasps)
Size: Up to ⅝"
Range: Central and eastern United States
Habitat: Deciduous woodlands, logs, fields, wooden structures

Black Carpenter Ants are large ants that form complex colonies in some form of wood source. They do not eat the wood, but chew it away for nesting cavities. Colonies consist of different types of Black Carpenter Ants, including a queen and different-size workers. In general they have the familiar ant-like constricted waist region and clearly elbowed antennae. They are colored jet black and have yellowish hairs on their abdomen. They feed on just about anything, including a wide variety of insects, aphid honeydew, fungi, fruits, and scraps from humans (especially sweets). A scout ant, upon finding a food source, leaves a chemical trail back to the nest to notify others where to go. It is best not to handle these ants, as they can deliver a painful bite.

Bumble Bees, *Bombus* spp.
Order: Hymenoptera (Ants, Bees, and Wasps)
Size: Up to ¾"
Range: Throughout most of the United States, especially northern latitudes
Habitat: Open woodlands, gardens, fields

Bumble bees are easily recognized by their large, robust bodies, which are covered in long fine hairs, and their lazy "bumbling" flight. Like ants and wasps, they have a very thin waist (pedicel), but it is obscured by hair, giving them a plump look. Their color is yellow overall, except for a black head and a black band between the wings. Female workers have specialized rear legs with a shiny, concave basket for transporting pollen. Bumble bees are extremely important ecologically as pollinators of a wide variety of flowering plants. Worker bees forage away from the nest (which is placed on the ground or in a depression), where they drink flower nectar for energy and collect pollen that is made into honey to feed the young. They are not aggressive, and although they can sting, they rarely do except as a last resort in self-defense.

Honeybees, *Apis* spp.
Order: Hymenoptera (Ants, Bees, and Wasps)
Size: Up to ⅝"
Range: Throughout North America
Habitat: Open woodlands, fields, orchards, gardens

Native to Europe, honeybees were introduced to North America in the 1800s and are now well established around the world. They are extremely important as pollinators of all kinds of flowering plants and commercial crops and for their production of honey and wax. Their hives are located in hollow trees or man-made boxes, where there is a complex social structure of queens, domestic males (drones), and thousands of worker females. They all have two sets of membranous wings, a very thin waist region, and elbowed antennae. Their color is reddish brown, with distinctive yellow and black bands on the nearly hairless abdomen. Workers use specialized rear legs with a "basket" to transport pollen and a crop to store nectar, both of which help to feed the colony. These bees can deliver a painful sting if threatened, and a barb on the stinger causes it to lodge into its victim and ultimately kill the bee.

Western Yellowjacket, *Vespula pensylvanica*
Order: Hymenoptera (Ants, Bees, and Wasps)
Size: Up to ½"
Range: Western half of North America
Habitat: Fields, woodland edges, rural yards

Yellowjackets are a kind of wasp, in a different group than the hairy, pollen-collecting bees (even though they are sometimes called "meat bees"). The Western Yellowjacket has a stout, smooth body with two pairs of grayish transparent wings and a distinct black-and-yellow banded abdomen. They are scavengers for all types of food, including meat, and eat a variety of insects, slugs, and nectar. They form colonies centered about a chambered, papery nest found on buildings, on trees, or in the ground. The nest is made of digested wood pulp, and new nests are built each year. Females are capable of stinging multiple times and are easily provoked. Bites are not serious, unless the victim has an allergy to the venom. The Western Yellowjacket is nearly identical to the Eastern Yellowjacket of the eastern United States.

OTHER
INVERTEBRATES

Black Widow, *Latrodectus mactans*
Order: Araneae (Spiders)
Size: Up to ⅜" (females larger than males)
Range: Throughout the United States
Habitat: Dark, hidden areas in woodpiles, sheds, debris

The Black Widow is one of the most feared spiders due to its secretive but dangerous nature. Although their bites are rarely fatal, they can cause serious illness. The female is glossy black with a large, rounded abdomen; medium-length legs; and a bright red, hourglass-shaped spot on her underside (this may appear as two separate red lines divided by black). The male has a much smaller body but relatively long legs and is paler in color with dull reddish marks on his abdomen. Both sexes are capable of injecting venom, but the female gives a larger volume. They feed on insects or other spiders that become ensnared in their webs, whereby they wrap the prey in silk and ingest the juices. Oftentimes the female will eat the male after mating. The underside of the female is illustrated.

American House Spider, *Parasteatoda tepidariorum*
Order: Araneae (Spiders)
Size: Up to ¼" (females larger than males)
Range: Throughout the United States
Habitat: Houses, barns, sheds, and other buildings

This common spider is a member of the group known as "cobweb weavers" or "comb-footed spiders" because of the irregular webs they weave and the presence of comb-like bristles on the ends of the hind legs. As with most spiders, the American House Spider has a small cephalothorax (head and thorax combined) that bears four pairs of walking legs and a larger, bulbous abdomen (especially large in females). This spider has no antennae, and its mouthparts are flanked by a pair of small sharp fangs. Its color is light brown with variable blackish and gray patches and mottling on the abdomen. When prey is trapped in the web, this spider will encase it with extra silk and often carry it to another location to suck out the fluids. They generally avoid humans and run away or feign death if disturbed, but rough handling could result in a minor but painful bite. The female is illustrated.

Banded Garden Spider, *Argiope trifasciata*
Order: Araneae (Spiders)
Size: Up to 1" (females larger than males)
Range: Throughout the United States
Habitat: Gardens, grassy fields, thickets

Also known as the Banded Argiope, this spider is in the group known as the "orb-weavers" because their webs are composed of round, spiraling rings of silk suspended between grasses and shrubs. Its abdomen is elongate and pointy at the rear. Its legs are fairly long and, when at rest, are held with the front two pairs forward and the back two pairs behind. Females have a creamy or yellow abdomen with thin black bands and a fuzzy, grayish carapace. Males are substantially smaller than females and have a pale gray, gold-speckled abdomen. The spider's web is up to 2 feet across; it builds it early in the morning and subsequently eats it at the close of day. It makes a new web each morning. Banded Garden Spiders wait in the center of their web, head down, for any insects flying or jumping into it, whereby they wrap the prey in silk and suck out the juices. They can deliver a bite if harassed or if they sense that their eggs are in danger. The female is illustrated.

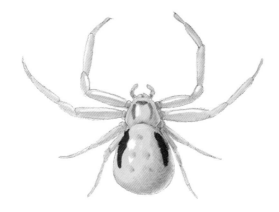

Goldenrod Crab Spider, *Misumena vatia*

Order: Araneae (Spiders)
Size: Up to ⅜" (females larger than males)
Range: Throughout the United States
Habitat: Areas with flowering plants; gardens, fields

The Goldenrod Crab Spider is a member of the group known as "crab spiders" because it typically holds its legs out to the sides of its body, like crabs, and prefer to crawl sideways more than forward or backward. The first two pairs of legs are noticeably longer than the hind two and are held out for grasping prey. The color of its body can change to match its surroundings, from whitish to bright yellow (like the goldenrod flower), and there are usually red marks on either side of its abdomen and between its eyes. The male is smaller than the female, with a small abdomen but proportionately longer legs, and has a brownish body with a pale spot on the center of its carapace. This species is considered a "flower spider," those that do not spin a web but climb onto plants and flowers waiting to ambush visiting insects (especially pollinators). Goldenrod Crab Spiders are harmless to humans. The female is illustrated.

Bold Jumping Spider, *Phidippus audax*
Order: Araneae (Spiders)
Size: Up to ⅝"
Range: Throughout the United States
Habitat: Gardens, fields, open woodlands

The jumping spiders are a group of small, hairy, compact, short-legged spiders with an incredible jumping ability. They also have four pairs of eyes, two of which are large and forward facing, giving them highly developed stereo vision. The Bold Jumping Spider is quite large for a jumping spider and is colored mostly black, with scattered white and gray markings (juveniles have orange on their abdomen). The chelicerae (front fangs) are iridescent bluish green. These spiders are active during the day, especially in bright light, when they can use their keen vision to locate prey. They set a silken tagline and leap at their victims, even those in flight. If the spider misses the target, it can climb its way back via the tagline. It eats insects and other spiders, even those much larger than itself.

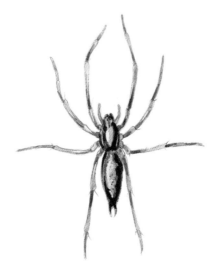

Grass Spiders, *Agelenopsis* spp.

Order: Araneae (Spiders)
Size: Up to ¾"
Range: Throughout the United States
Habitat: Gardens, grassy fields

The grass spider, several species of which exist in North America, is a member of the group known as "tunnel weavers," who weave a flat web in grasses with a funnel-shaped section to one side, where the spider waits for prey. When a prey insect ensnares in the web, the spider scurries out to inject it with venom and carries it back into the funnel section to feed. Grass spiders are cryptically colored in browns and grays, with a light tan cephalothorax that has two darker brown stripes and a mottled gray, teardrop-shaped abdomen, which terminates in pointed spinnerets (the silk-producing organs). The legs are long and thin. Grass spiders are harmless to humans, being shy and retreating to safety when encountered.

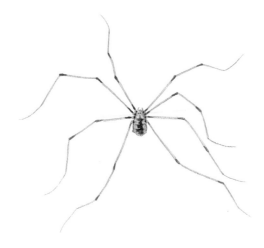

Striped Daddy Long-legs, *Leiobunum vittatum*

Order: Opiliones (Harvestmen)
Size: Up to ¼"
Range: Central and eastern United States
Habitat: Woodlands, gardens, shrubbery

These curious arachnids are not true spiders, but belong to a group known as harvestman spiders. Many species occur in North America, and most have a distinctive oval, flattened body with a broadly fused head, thorax, and abdomen and extremely long, thin legs. Despite the long legs, they are held bent and the body stays close to the ground. Like spiders, harvestmen have eight legs, but the second pair is longer than the others and is often used in sensory perception. Striped Daddy Long-legs have a pale body with dark stripes down their back and blackish legs. They feed on decaying plant material or small insects and will often congregate in clusters on the warm sides of buildings or tree trunks. Contrary to some myths, harvestmen have very small feeding pincers, are nonvenomous, and are completely harmless to humans. They easily break off a leg in self-defense that will not regenerate.

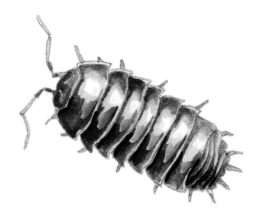

Sow Bugs (many species)

Order: Isopoda (Sow Bugs and Allies)
Size: Up to ½"
Range: Throughout the United States
Habitat: Moist places under rocks and logs; gardens, woodlands

The large group of invertebrates that includes sow bugs (also known as "wood lice") are not insects but crustaceans, being related to the crabs and lobsters. They are small and oblong, with a flattened carapace composed of several segments. They have seven pairs of legs of nearly equal length; tiny, simple eyes; and two taillike projections (uropods). Their color is some shade of gray or brown. Some species can roll their bodies into a tight ball and are known as "pill bugs" or "roly-polies." Sow bugs stay in secluded, dark, damp places during the day and venture out at night to feed on plants, leaves, and decaying organic matter with chewing mouthparts. The eggs are carried in brood pouches on the underside of females and hatch to young that look like miniature adults.

Garden Snail, *Helix aspersa*
Class: Gastropoda (Snails and Slugs)
Size: Shell 1¼" diameter
Range: Throughout North America
Habitat: Shady or moist areas, gardens, croplands

Garden Snails were introduced from Europe and are now widespread in North America. This is the snail you are most likely to see in your garden. The body is like a gray slug with a thin, spiraled, brown shell with darker brown or black bands and striations. When the snail is active, the long foot, head, and two sets of tentacles are extended, but the soft parts quickly retract into the shell if threatened. During very dry weather snails can survive by contracting into their shell and sealing their bottom with mucus. They are mostly active at night or during the day during wet weather, feeding on a wide variety of plants with a rasping tongue. Though these are not the typical snail used as escargot in cuisine, they are still edible and considered a delicacy by some.

Leopard Slug, *Limax maximus*
Class: Gastropoda (Snails and Slugs)
Size: Up to 6"
Range: Throughout North America
Habitat: Woodlands, gardens, urban areas

Also known as the "spotted garden slug," this species is indigenous to Europe but is now common and widespread in North America and is the slug you are most likely to see under rocks and scraps of wood in your backyard. Its body is grayish or brown, with black "leopard spots" on the mantle and broken black lines along the sides and lower back. The slug has a long, muscular foot and two sets of retractable tentacles on its head that it uses for smelling and light detection. The posterior of its body is wrinkled and slightly keeled. Leopard Slugs feed on plants, decaying organic material, and mushrooms and are sometimes pests in gardens. They lay a mass of clear, round eggs that develop directly into small slugs. Active at night, they become dormant in times of dry weather.

Black Slug, *Arion ater*
Class: Gastropoda (Snails and Slugs)
Size: Up to 6"
Range: Pacific Northwest
Habitat: Moist fields, gardens

The Black Slug is a large slug introduced from Europe and is now common in the northwestern United States. The body is elongate and broad, with a rounded back and blunt tail section. The front half of the body is topped by a raised mantle covered in small tubercles, while the back half has long, linear ridges. As with other slugs, the Black Slug has a pair of long, light-sensing tentacles; a pair of shorter smelling tentacles; and a tough foot that runs the length of its underside for locomotion. The color of its mucous-covered skin is generally jet black, but variants may be whitish or brownish. Young slugs are colored tan or reddish but attain darker colors with maturity. Black Slugs are active mostly during the wetness and coolness of night, feeding on plants, fungi, and decaying organic matter, and can be a pest to crops and gardens.

Earthworms (many species)
Class: Oligochaeta (Earthworms)
Size: ½–14"
Range: Throughout North America
Habitat: Moist soils and compost; under logs and rocks

The class of earthworms consists of well over a thousand species, but they all share a similar body plan even if their size varies considerably. Essentially, they are like segmented tubes, tapered at both ends, with a mucus-covered skin (cuticle) and very simple internal organs and sensory apparatus. They make tunnels through soil by pushing aside the soil or by ingesting it and expelling the remains behind (one can see little piles of these remains, called castings, near a tunnel entrance). For grip, they are lined with tiny, tough bristles that stick to the soil, and wavelike contractions move the body forward. All earthworms are very beneficial to soil health because they increase aeration and release partially digested organic matter that plant roots easily absorb. Earthworms reproduce by coupling together at an enlarged band (the clitellum) and produce small egg capsules. The Red Wriggler, *Eisenia fetida*, is illustrated.

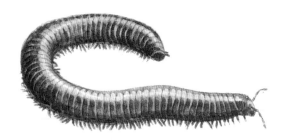

Millipedes (many species)
Class: Diplopoda (Millipedes)
Size: Up to 4"
Range: Throughout North America
Habitat: Under rocks and logs around moist soils and leaf litter

The familiar and friendly millipedes are part of a group of invertebrates known as myriapods, which also includes the centipedes. They have long, cylindrical or flattened bodies with many hardened, thin segments, most of which bear two pairs of tiny legs. The word *millipede* means "thousand legs," and although this is an exaggeration, species with over a hundred legs are not uncommon (the record is 752 legs!). After hatching, most millipedes have only three pairs of legs, and with each molt more legs are added. They are relatively slow moving on land and mostly burrow through soil headed by a tough shield behind the head and propelled by the force of their many legs. Millipedes feed on decaying organic matter and plants and, like earthworms, are important for the health of soils. They do not bite or sting, thus are completely harmless to humans. In defense, they crawl away, twist into a compact spiral, or roll into a ball like a pill bug. The American Giant Millipede, *Narceus americanus*, is illustrated.

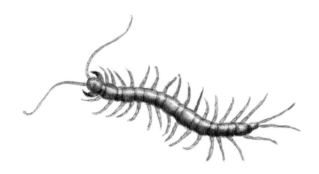

Centipedes (many species)
Class: Chilopoda (Centipedes)
Size: Up to 1¾"
Range: Throughout North America
Habitat: Under rocks and logs around moist soils and leaf litter

Centipedes are in the same group (myriapods) as millipedes, but they have only one pair of legs for each body segment (millipedes have two pairs per segment). The name *centipede* means "hundred legs," but in actuality the amount can vary from just over a dozen to well over a hundred. Their body is highly segmented and flattened, allowing them great mobility and the ability to squeeze into tight areas. They run quite fast and use their tactile antennae as their key method of perception. Centipedes are very sensitive to desiccation, so they are restricted to moist areas and are normally active at night. They are predators on other invertebrates, including insects, spider, slugs, and worms, which they seize with venom-laced claws near the head. If handled roughly, they can give a painful but nonserious bite. The Stone Centipede, *Lithobius forficatus*, is illustrated.

Index

Index

Index

Index

About the Author/Illustrator

Todd Telander is a naturalist/illustrator/
artist living in Walla Walla, Washington.
He has studied and illustrated wildlife
since 1989 while living in California,
Colorado, New Mexico, and Washington. He graduated from the University
of California, Santa Cruz, with degrees
in biology, environmental studies,
and scientific illustration, and has
since illustrated numerous books and
other publications, including books in
FalconGuides' Scats and Tracks series. His wife, Kirsten Telander, is
a writer, and they have two sons, Miles and Oliver. His work can be
viewed online at toddtelander.com or telandergallery.com.